YOU GOTTA GET UP

YOU GOTTA GET UP

GRAB HOLD OF YOUR LIFE
AFTER BEING KNOCKED DOWN,
HELD BACK, AND LEFT OUT

REAL TALK KIM

EMANATE
BOOKS

Published in Nashville, Tennessee, by Emanate Books, an imprint of Thomas Nelson. Emanate Books and Thomas Nelson are registered trademarks of HarperCollins Christian Publishing, Inc.

Author is represented by the literary agency of The FEDD Agency, Inc., Post Office Box 341973, Austin, Texas 78734.

ISBN 978-1-4002-4199-6 (eBook)
ISBN 978-1-4002-4198-9 (TP)

Library of Congress Control Number: 2023934154

Printed in the United States of America

23 24 25 26 27 LBC 6 5 4 3 2

CONTENTS

PART IV: FREEDOM LOOKS GOOD ON YOU

INTRODUCTION

I look at pain like a disco ball. I look at rejection like a disco ball. I look at sadness like a disco ball. Pain can break you into a thousand pieces—and no one wants that; however, God can take those broken pieces and create a beautiful mosaic that shines. Everyone wants to be a diamond, but no one wants to get cut. Even though the pain we walk through may not be our fault, the healing is our responsibility. And if we don't heal, we will bleed on people who never cut us.

I really believe that God sometimes breaks our spirits to save our souls. When you've been praying for something, you may feel discouraged because the enemy is lying to you, telling you that God isn't there for you and that you will never receive your heart's desire. But you must remember that God's timing is very different from ours.

Think about rejection. Rejection isn't necessarily the result of some person's strategically wanting out of your life; it is often the result of God's taking someone out of your future. The rejection is the release.

I have personally walked this out in my latest season. When the devil is trying to put you down, to shut you up, to make your life null and void, God will use the enemy's plots to move you where He wants you. God won't let the enemy keep you down on His watch.

Each chapter of this book will end with a declaration of freedom and an opportunity for you to spend a moment to pray with me. Think about each declaration and then determine if you are ready for the next chapter. Give Jesus the freedom to assist you as you move along on your journey. Don't get frustrated if it takes you a minute to get there. Even after I made the decision to change my life, I moved in with my parents and had no idea I would be there five years. It may take you a much shorter time than it did me. You can be your very best friend in this journey by opening up and being honest with yourself.

When we know that God sees us in our brokenness and has a plan to bring good out of it, we can be encouraged to get close to Him during difficult seasons. Don't agree with the enemy by speaking negative words over your life! *You gotta get up!* It's the secret to allowing God to work in your heart. Just get up one more time than you fall down.

REAL TALK KIM

PART I
REAL-LIFE RESILIENCE

God did not promise life would be easy. God promised that He would never leave us nor forsake us. His promise is that He will be with us until the very end. Because of this promise, we will not only be able to face each new crisis but also overcome the pain that goes along with it.

RADICAL RESTORATION

I found Pastor Kim in June 2021. I was six months postseparation and, one month prior, had learned that my best friend, confidante, and support person had betrayed me and hijacked my life! She left her husband for mine. Literally! She left her home, her kids, and her husband, and moved in with mine and started planning a new life with him.

I had never in my life felt that level of hurt, betrayal, confusion, and pure grief.

I would lie in my bed clenching the blankets, curled up in the fetal position, praying! I would tell God, "If this isn't going to get any better, any easier, then please, Lord, let me die!!" But, then I would wake up the next morning.

I started listening to the prayer calls on Facebook Live and plugged into the Inner Circle. I had already read Kim's books *Shut Hell Up* and *Beautifully Broken*. I knew the voice of Pastor Kim was going to be crucial in my healing process. She was someone who had been there and was able to overcome! I am so thankful to God that she did the hard work, obeyed the voice of the Lord, and walked out of her mess in faith even when she, too, wanted to die. Thank you, PK, for doing the hard things when it isn't easy! Thank you for listening to and obeying the voice of the Lord and paving the way for so many! Thank you, God, for this incredible pastor and mentor who truly does do life with us! I pray fresh strength, endurance, wisdom, grace, and anointing be poured out upon her continuously, Lord, as she continues to obey Your voice and walk bravely in her calling transparently before the world. Love you, Pastor Kim! I appreciate you so much. Hopefully one day we will meet, and you will feel it in the hug I will be giving you.

—R

Chapter 1

CHOOSE YOUR HARD

Your life doesn't get better by chance, it gets
better by change!

—RTK

Are you in a place that you hate? How long do you want to stay there? Are you where you thought you would be at this point in your life? Are you the person you had hoped to be by now? Change is hard. Staying stuck is hard. But, let's be honest, it takes the same amount of time, energy, and effort to remain in the "stuckness" as it does to forge a new path.

Stuckness, the inability to change or go forward, is a mindset that will rule your life and detour you from your destiny. So, join me on the journey of choosing your hard. We don't have the promise of an easy life, but with God we do have the promise of a victorious one!

When you say you're stuck, what are you really feeling? It could be rooted in the emotion of fear, and fear will immobilize you. Sometimes fear is well-founded and easy to pinpoint, but sometimes it is outside of our awareness. It can be fear of failure, fear of being alone, fear of sickness and pain. Fear can breed frustration, despair, and doubt. Let's be honest and determine the reason we are stuck and can't move in either direction. Is it because of fear?

"I, KIMBERLY ANN JONES, AM A SURVIVOR OF STUCKNESS."

I spent so much time trying to figure out why I allowed labels to define me.

Why was I dependent on others' approval?

Why did I always choose the ones who rejected me?

Why did I allow all these things to keep me stuck when I could have just gotten up and moved on?

We can be so imprisoned by our emotional baggage that we become defensive or resistant to change. We refuse to move in either direction. We can't imagine a life other than the broken life we are experiencing, so it's easier to withdraw than to create a new life.

Sound familiar? This is where discontentment and depression set in. We become stagnant. We don't realize that it is as easy to move forward as it is to stay stuck! Too often we hope the issues we face will resolve themselves on their own, without any effort on our part.

It would take too much work to figure life out. That's the type of thinking often reeling through our minds. But with a little effort and thought, you can turn your life around. You can choose a new future and start walking in that direction.

The *and* is up to *you*! It's time for you to move forward.

It's easy to become consumed with the past. But if you don't let go of your past, your past won't let you live! It's easy to fail to move forward because fear has set in and become the norm. Instead of being imprisoned by the pain of the past, just ask, *"And?"*

> He filed for divorce. *And?*
> My promotion fell through. *And?*
> I got fired. *And?*
> They lied about me. *And?*
> The *and* is up to *you*! It's time for you to move forward.
> *You gotta get up!*

"THAT WOULD NEVER WORK FOR ME."

Stuckness will have you saying "never" for the rest of your life:

> I could never do it.
> I could never go there.
> I could never accomplish that.

I could never get that job promotion. I'm not qualified.
I could never get married. I'm not ready to answer to
anyone else.

Well, why not? You're uncertain and frustrated. You've
stayed up at night worrying about your tomorrow. What
voices have you listened to that have determined your
present situation?

You're afraid. *Of what?*
You're confused. *About what?*

Every word you speak to yourself either strengthens
or weakens your behavior. Where your mind goes, your
body will follow. It's most important to get honest with
yourself.

I am in constant communication with myself as I quote
favorite scriptures from the Bible. It's my choice to determine my altitude daily. I can allow life's challenges to deter
my judgment and cause me to see a glass half empty or
make the choice to see it half full. While words can tear you
down, they can also build you up. I am a prime example
of allowing a season of loss to cloud my judgment, which
then caused me to focus on negatives instead of realizing
that "I can do all things through Christ who strengthens
me" (Philippians 4:13 NKJV). I had no idea that a job loss
would open doors to an even more secure job opportunity.
All it took was a decision to get up one more time than I
fell down.

Kind words are like honey—
sweet to the soul and healthy for the body.

(PROVERBS 16:24)

Watch your tongue and keep your mouth shut,
and you will stay out of trouble.

(PROVERBS 21:23)

When you realize your identity is not wrapped up in whatever caused your pain (for example, your divorce, abortion, bankruptcy, rape), your greatest humiliation and frustration can become the point of your greatest elevation. Who could have known that I would be mentoring thousands of people today as I became transparent about my own pain and foolish decisions that set me up to determine it was time for a lifestyle change? How long have you been sabotaging your future because of your past? It's time to recognize that there is purpose in your pain. The difficult experiences that cause brokenness always have a way of pushing you higher. The devil hasn't been fighting you because you're weak. He's fighting you because he knows just how strong you are.

If you had told me ten years ago that I would be a life coach, a mentor, an international speaker, and a pastor, I would have immediately stopped the conversation. I could never have seen my life as it is today. I had lived a life with many labels: learning disabled, divorcée, single mom, disconnected daughter, a failure. I was always trying to prove my worth, and it seemed I always connected to those who

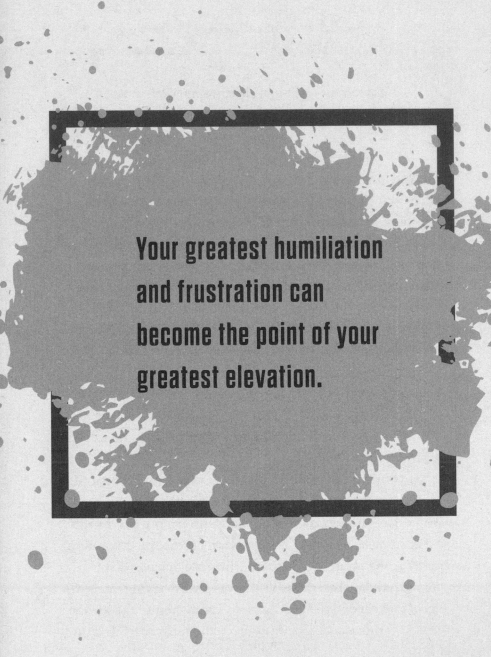

Your greatest humiliation and frustration can become the point of your greatest elevation.

were trying to change me to fit their mold. I was full of insecurities while trying to find that niche that would identify me as successful, powerful, secure, and prosperous. I had the need to control everything in my life, including my relationships and my business. And yet, even though it worked for a little while, I still found myself lacking and discontent.

At thirty-six years old, I moved back into my mom and dad's home with my two young sons. I had no income and no idea what my next season of life would look like. My marriage had failed and I felt like *I* was a failure. I was the only one in my family who could not keep a marriage together. I was too traumatized by my own pain to understand the pain and anger that my two boys were experiencing at the time. I wondered why I was sentenced by the jury of my past failures to the very home that I had worked so feverishly at eighteen to escape. Returning home as a failure was the most horrendous sentence that could ever have been handed down to me, or so I thought.

At age eighteen, I had fled the control and oversight of my family because I believed I was ready for independence and didn't need anyone to give me direction. That idea really is hilarious when I look back and realize that my parents were always there for me—sending money when needed, buying me cars, and even buying milk for my babies. Yet, I told myself how great it was to be out of the controlling arms of the same ones who never let me down.

How many times had I said that living near my parents would never work? Yet, the season of being back home with my mom and dad was one of the most maturing and strengthening seasons of my life. I told myself it would never work, but it proved me wrong by working in my favor.

"I DON'T HAVE TIME TO MAKE A CHANGE."

When something happens that we don't understand and can't control, God understands it. He already knew it was coming and determined beforehand that He would use it to wake us up.

Before my marriage fell apart, I was so busy balancing the "act" that I called my life that I did not realize the consistency of my failed decisions. I told myself I did not have time to make changes that could have changed the trajectory of my future and my family's. I was too busy doing whatever was necessary to bring in money to make the next month's mortgage payment.

You see, we had recently moved. And the new home I had selected was in a pricey gated subdivision that I thought would impress everyone. I did not consider that I was the primary breadwinner and our ability to stay in that home depended on my success. At that time, it seemed that there was favor on everything I touched.

But then my marriage began to fail. My life partner, who had vowed to be there until "death do us part," had totally disconnected from our family.

I was certain that I did not have time to worry about me; everything and everybody was depending on my next move. Not only did I think I didn't have time for change, but I was too weary to figure out how to change. Emotionally, I could not keep it together anymore.

"IT'S TOO LATE FOR ME."

As long as you have a pulse, God has a plan.

Consider the Samaritan woman who met Jesus at a well. Jesus told His disciples that He needed to go through Samaria on His way to Galilee. Jesus did not have an apparent pressing need to linger in Samaria, yet He knew there was a woman who would come to the well, be open to His words, and believe (John 4).

In those days, the Jews despised the Samaritans. The Samaritans saw this woman as an outcast because she had been married five times and was currently living with a man who was not her husband. She came to the well in the middle of the day to avoid the gossipers who gathered in the cool of the evening. I'm sure she believed that it was too late for her to change, and she was stuck not knowing how to make her life better. Most of the other women could not relate to her lifestyle, and I'm sure they didn't trust her around their husbands. Then this man, Jesus, met her at the well.

> As long as you have a pulse, God has a plan.

She was shocked that a Jewish man would speak to her. But God had a plan. It was ordained by God that she meet Jesus face-to-face.

I easily relate to this story because I, too, felt rejected and betrayed by so many when I returned to my childhood home. I knew people were talking about my failures, so it was easiest to avoid anyone I had known in the past. In my worst moment of despair, Jesus let me know that I was to live as though I had no past and He would justify me. I realized that I would need to get up every day and face life instead of allowing failure to hold me hostage. There was no one in my past who would bail me out of my life losses, yet I was allowing those people to determine my present decisions. As I slowly began to let go of the influence of my past, it became easier each day to look toward the future. The miracle was that when I did meet some of my child-hood friends, I could look them in the eye and speak with all sincerity because I knew God had forgiven me and I had also forgiven myself.

Isn't it amazing that we can stumble into miracles—that people like you, me, and the Samaritan woman can meet Jesus?

> O LORD, you have examined my heart
>   and know everything about me.
> You know when I sit down or stand up.
>   You know my thoughts even when I'm
>   far away.
> You see me when I travel
>   and when I rest at home.
> You know everything I do.
>
> (PSALM 139:1–3)

"I'M EXHAUSTED. I'M JUST TOO TIRED."

The Samaritan woman's meeting with Jesus was not a chance encounter. It had been arranged long before she made her first bad choice. After she met Jesus, she would have to choose her path going forward. This Jewish man told her everything about her life. He knew she had been married five times and was not living with a husband presently. Although He was accurate about her life, He was not condescending. She realized that He was more than just a man. She was sick and tired of her life. What if this man could offer her a way out?

> The woman said, "I know the Messiah is coming—the one who is called Christ. When he comes, he will explain everything to us." Then Jesus told her, "I AM the Messiah!" (John 4:25–26)

"IT'S EASIER TO COAST ON NEUTRAL."

Picture this woman's life that day before she went to the well. She was living with a man out of wedlock, had no friends, just one man after the other. She was used to the dysfunctional life she had created. Then Jesus came along and offered her an alternative to her endless coasting.

Part of what keeps us from moving past our traumas is the belief that we have no future. But God always has a plan, and that plan is to do us good and not harm, to give us a future and a hope.

"For I know the plans I have for you," says the LORD. "They are plans for good and not for disaster, to give you a future and a hope. In those days when you pray, I will listen. If you look for me wholeheartedly, you will find me." (Jeremiah 29:11–13)

"I CAN'T GET UNSTUCK BECAUSE . . ."

I've made so many unwise decisions.
I'm so calloused and hardened because of hidden sins.
It's easier for me to forgive others than it is to forgive myself.

Are these some of your thoughts as you face each new day?

The woman at the well knew the entire city had heard about her past and no one believed she could change. Then this Jewish man came to the well and offered her hope. After realizing that she could get unstuck and be forgiven for all she had done, this woman ran back into her town and told everyone to come and see a man who knew everything she had done. She risked the whole town laughing at her and ridiculing her, but she didn't care. This woman had gotten out of bed that morning weary and stuck in her seemingly endless routine, and now she was announcing to everyone who had judged her that they needed to meet the man who had given her hope.

If Jesus Christ would set this unnamed woman free of her guilt, consider giving Him a chance as we take this journey together. Stuckness will not be your destination any longer!

GETTING UP!

DECLARATION

I once thought I would always be imprisoned in the chains of my own making. Now I know I can release everything that has kept me bound. I will no longer allow myself or others to imprison me with negative thoughts. Just as the Samaritan woman at the well accepted freedom from the labels that had kept her bound, I release everything that will attempt to keep me from my focus on freedom.

PRAYER

Jesus,
It's a new day in You. I will, at the end of this journey with Real Talk Kim, find the freedom You have promised me. I will walk as a new person in new shoes and will not attempt to return to those things that have kept me stuck.
Amen.

RADICAL RESTORATION

My friend introduced me to you, Real Talk Kim. I love how hilarious you are. I can relate to being married several times and messing up as a parent. I can relate to being raised in church and going to church all the time, including revivals. I had a cleft palate from birth, struggled in school with learning, and was picked on by bullies in school. I always felt like my parents only loved my older brother and younger sister. We dealt with family curses like anger and abuse. I now have started trusting and believing in God to answer my prayers to save both my boys. One is a drug addict and the other one has an addiction as well. I have asked God to

help me pull the layers of hurt, pain, and rejection off me, and I am willing to do what He wants me to do. I lost my grandmother and dad within two months and am learning to mourn and move, as you say. I am trying to grow in God. I am learning to communicate with my husband. I am trying to listen to you and my pastor. I know I must take one step at a time. Thank you for being real and telling us like it is.

—S

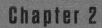

Chapter 2

STUCKNESS

Unforgiveness is choosing to stay trapped in a jail cell of bitterness, serving time for someone else's crime.

—AUTHOR UNKNOWN

Stop *living the lie that others speak against you.*

Has anyone ever told you that you were never going to succeed, never going to find a life partner, never going to _____ (fill in the blank)? Did you allow yourself to believe them? How did that work for you? Not great, right? But what does God say about you?

> "For I know the plans I have for you," says the LORD. "They are plans for good and not for disaster, to give you a future and a hope." (Jeremiah 29:11)

When we believe what others say about us, that becomes our reality, rather than what God says about us. We can be more concerned with what people think about us than what God knows about us.

Why allow a lie to distract you from your destiny? Ignore the voices speaking doubt and hate, and allow God to work all things together for your good.

I have had several "worst seasons" in my life, but each time when I finally came to the end of myself, I realized that only God could work out those good things for me. After that point, I was able to turn my messes from each season into messages that now help change thousands of lives daily.

STUCK ON PETTY

It's so easy to be petty today, now that our society is ruled by social media platforms. You see your friend's post one hour after you have an argument, and you just know the entire post is about you. The whole world is going to read the post and will know it's about you, right? Hey, what if you could just let it go? What if you chose to forgive and move on instead of holding on to it? Don't be a Petty Betty, who majors on the minor issues of life.

You have options and you have the freedom of choice. You can decide to post your own feelings on social media for everyone to see. Or you can consider that maybe, just maybe, something else was bothering your friend and it wasn't even about you. Or perhaps it really was about you, but something terrible happened in your friend's life that you don't know about, and you just ended up being the fall guy for their emotions.

Please understand, the world doesn't stop and start on our feelings. Our good day or bad day will not stop the earth from turning on its axis. Tomorrow is going to happen whether we like it or not.

Pettiness is being intentionally attentive to trivial details. *Trivial* details. Don't let trivial details affect your relationships. Determine that you will be the one to choose the higher ground. Be the bigger person. Stop the cycle. Don't be moved by small things that won't matter before long.

God created us for relationships, and it takes both parties to make a relationship work. Through Christ, we can have better relationships with those around us. When the apostle Peter wrote that love covers a multitude of sins, he was letting us know that we all would make mistakes in relationships and would need forgiveness continually. When we realize we are imperfect people living in an imperfect world, it helps us understand others because we are honest with ourselves.

> Most important of all, continue to show deep love for each other, for love covers a multitude of sins. (1 Peter 4:8)

In my life journey I have had several Petty Bettys who seemed to encourage my brokenness more than my journey to wholeness. As I finally came to the decision to make a move in my life, not just for my personal good but for the good of my two boys, I realized that the so-called friends who had been with me for many years could not go with me into my new season. They had been supporting me as

I made stupid decisions about family, jobs, and especially about God. My journey forward could not include them.

I had no idea what my new season would look like, and I was afraid of the unknown—just as most of you are. I had left the comfort of home at eighteen because I wanted independence; however, independence had not served me well. My idea of independence was to live emotionally disconnected from home and family and prove to the world that I was capable of succeeding on my own. It's amazing how the enemy can set you up for failure and you walk along in agreement without even realizing you are on a destructive path.

It may not take you as long as it did me to come to the end of yourself. It took me thirty-six years of trying to prove my worth to finally realize that everyone needs someone to help them along. That someone needs to be on your side and ready to fight with you until the very end. That someone must be honest and tell you the truth about yourself for you to begin your journey of freedom.

STUCK ON DISOBEDIENCE

Lot's wife was a prime example of a person who sabotaged her own future. She proved to be a powerful example of someone who did not understand the meaning of obedience. The book of Genesis describes the punishment she received for her desire to be independent of God's instruction.

When they were safely out of the city, one of the angels ordered, "Run for your lives! And don't look back or stop anywhere in the valley! Escape to the mountains, or you will be swept away!" . . .

But Lot's wife looked back as she was following behind him, and she turned into a pillar of salt. (Genesis 19:17, 26)

The story began when two angels arrived in Sodom, the town where Lot and his family lived. As was customary when visitors arrived in town, Lot invited them to spend the night at his house. The men of Sodom, who were caught up in sexual sin, began harassing Lot about releasing these angels to them. Instead, Lot offered his own daughters to the men to use as they pleased. They rejected the offer. These men were driven by lust and would not accept the women as a token exchange. Their lust was so powerful that nothing but the men (the angels) would satisfy.

God wanted His righteous people to get out before He destroyed the whole city:

Meanwhile, the angels questioned Lot. "Do you have any other relatives here in the city?" they asked. "Get them out of this place—your sons-in-law, sons, daughters, or anyone else. For we are about to destroy this city completely. The outcry against this place is so great it has reached the LORD, and he has sent us to destroy it." (Genesis 19:12–13)

Previously, the Lord had told Abraham:

"I have heard a great outcry from Sodom and Gomorrah, because their sin is so flagrant. I am going down to see if their actions are as wicked as I have heard. If not, I want to know." (Genesis 18:20–21)

It still amazes me how God, in His mercy, would spare a small family. Abraham had asked God to spare the entire city if he could find even fifty righteous people. We know that the conversation finally ended when Abraham reached the number ten, and God said that He would not destroy the city for the sake of ten people. There were not even ten righteous among these cities, so Lot knew he would have to flee or be annihilated with the unrighteous. (Lot was a foreigner in the city and had not succumbed to the lustful, degenerate sins rampant at that time.)

As the crowd of men moved to break down Lot's door to get to the angels whom they thought were just men, God struck the men with blindness so they could not find the door. God was giving Lot the time needed to get his little family out of Sodom.

I cannot even imagine Lot's anguish as he tried to per-suade his sons-in-law to accompany his family out of the city. Lot knew God meant business. Yet, the sons-in-law, who were from that region, were dealing with the same spirit of sodomy as the rest of the men. The angels began rushing Lot, his wife, and two daughters out of the city before it was too late. The angels knew God would keep His word and soon destroy the city.

The angels first told Lot to flee to the mountains, but Lot asked that his family travel to Zoar, a nearby city. By the time they reached Zoar, the Lord began raining down sulfur on Sodom and Gomorrah. I will never judge Lot's wife for her next action—she heard the devastation taking place and looked back.

I wonder how many of us look back as we begin moving forward in our personal lives. We determine to make a change, then succumb to the wiles of the enemy when we feel weak. I think Lot's wife was already missing her previous life. In that moment of weakness, she immediately became a pillar of salt because the instructions were not to look back as they moved forward. Her destruction was a sign for others to realize that there are consequences when you are stuck in disobedience.

Can you imagine the sounds of the devastation as the cities of Sodom and Gomorrah went up in flames, and the people of those cities realized there was nowhere to hide? They had made a choice to live in sin. I'm sure they were screaming out in pain and even frustration at their choices while they watched everything, including their families, be destroyed. And in this anguishing process, they were also being destroyed. All because of disobedience.

How did Lot and his daughters determine to keep moving forward when the matriarch of their family was no longer with them? Sounds so easy until we are faced with the choice of change and leaving people and places behind.

STUCK ON BITTERNESS

We know that bitterness, just like disobedience, is a deep hurt that poisons the soul. When you cannot or will not let go of hurt, it begins to cloud your decisions and cripple you on your journey through life. Bitterness eats away at the vitality of your spiritual life like a cancer of the soul. And if you do not deal with the bitterness, it will eventually contaminate your roots and infect the fruit your life produces.

———————

I remember when my mother was diagnosed with rheumatoid arthritis and she began her healing journey. My mother is an avid reader and a dedicated disciple of Jesus Christ, so she began an in-depth search into the whys of her diagnosis. My grandmother had been stricken with the same disease when my mom was very young.

The memories of her mother's condition came flooding back as she remembered family members caring for her mother because she was unable to walk. She also remembered the day her mother received a miracle when a prayer cloth was laid on her body on a Sunday afternoon with the family gathered around in prayer. Her mother jumped out of the bed that she had not left for a very long time and ran through the house while praising Jesus for the miracle.

My mom knew she would need to find her way to her own miracle or be unable to walk if the arthritis took control. So, she began a spiritual journey of awareness to let go of anything she carried that could have caused such a disease to attack her body. It was a step-by-step process as she began releasing the hurt, pain, and unforgiveness that she carried.

My mother chose never to allow life's hurts and unforgiveness to rule her. She is our family's example of releasing anyone who ever meant malice toward her. Instead of cursing someone out of bitterness, she chose to bless them and move on. Today my mother is living an amazing life, even after caring for my dad until he passed of dementia, and she carries no pain in her body. There are no signs that she had ever had rheumatoid arthritis.

I watched my mom journey through unfaithful relationships and a lot of hurt. She was my knight in shining armor when I, too, faced unfaithfulness and needed a strong arm to assist me in moving forward. Because my dad and mom were in ministry, I listen attentively to my mom when seeking direction for restoring and maintaining wholesome relationships.

When a trusted friend betrayed my mom, she became very guarded and more secluded and private for a season, until she realized that God did not create us to live on an isolated island alone without friends. She learned that, even though one friend may betray you, there are many people who understand loyalty and trust. You forgive those who betray you and keep living your best life. You do not have to allow them back into the VIP section of your life, but you can forgive and move on.

> Look after each other so that none of you fails to receive the grace of God. Watch out that no poisonous root of bitterness grows up to trouble you, corrupting many. (Hebrews 12:15)

To receive the grace of God, we must weed out the root of bitterness. Bitterness comes into our lives in so many

We can become bitter instead of better.

ways. Through jealousy, anger, un-forgiveness, and even irritation, we can become bitter instead of better. Satan's plan is for us to become focused on situations that have wounded us and people who have done us wrong so that we are stuck in our past, unable to move forward.

———

After the loss of her two-year-old son, my grandmother became so emotionally broken that her grief robbed her family of years of peace and tranquility. She became addicted to prescription drugs—anything that would give her solace to be able to sleep through the night. She also slept most of the day, so she lost years of raising her children. As the oldest, my mom was forced to become the surrogate mother to her two siblings. She helped them in their schooling and homelife. She completely missed out on having normal teen years.

Mom did not begin dating until she was almost eighteen years old, but at the age of twenty, she married my dad, an evangelist in full-time ministry. They began traveling throughout the southern states and were typically only home two or three times a year. During those years, my brother and I were born. When it was time for us to begin school, they planted a new church. Life rolled on by as our little family was consumed with ministry.

Years later, my parents moved to Atlanta, Georgia, to be near our grandparents as they were getting older. Eventually, they moved in with us and we became a tri-generational family. Thirteen years later, my granddad passed, and my grandmother continued living with my dad and mom.

My mom had not realized she was carrying hurt and bitterness from her past. Although she was a good daughter who cared for her mother, there were times that she and my grandmother would disagree. They never had that best-friend type of relationship. My mom began reading about feelings you bury alive that never die. These feelings are shoved in the background, and you just keep on living. However, the repressed feelings never truly die, and there seems to always be tension of some sort hovering just below the surface. She read about diseases brought on by pent-up feelings that you don't deal with.

One night, my mom was sitting in a recliner reading about these feelings when she was overcome with emotion. She realized she was holding on to so many feelings against her mother and that was the reason they could get upset with each other so easily.

It was during this time that my mom was diagnosed with rheumatoid arthritis. Can you see why fear gripped her? Because my grandmother had used prescription drugs to relieve pain, my mom would not take any drugs prescribed by the doctor. She believed there was something else she could do. This was one reason she was studying so relentlessly about feelings and emotions.

Mom had told the Lord Jesus that she would be a good student of the Word and asked for revelation and wisdom regarding her illness. As she read about feelings, she knew that she needed to be cleansed of the emotions she had carried throughout her life. She was about fifty-five years old when she realized she needed freedom from resentment and feelings of abandonment from her childhood.

My mother was an excellent Bible teacher and pastor. She was the picture of perfection when it came to standing by her husband and our family. She was a wonderful daughter. But now it became clear she carried a lot of baggage from the past. It was time to unpack the baggage, let it all go, and allow Jesus to truly be Lord of her life.

She went into her mother's bedroom, knelt down by her little eighty-year-old mother, and asked her mother to work with her. She said, "Mom, I want you to forgive me for the bitterness I've held over feeling like you abandoned me when Randy [her brother] died. I was only seven years old, and I felt that I had lost my brother *and* my mother."

My grandmother, weeping, said, "I forgive you."

My mother asked her mom to forgive her for carrying feelings of rejection and remorse about their family not being normal. She explained that she had never realized how much pain my grandmother carried from past hurts and the loss of a child. This had resulted in a lifetime of sickness and regret and had caused our family's norm to be one of sickness and pain suffered through loss. For about an hour my mom and grandmother went through the process of offering and receiving forgiveness.

My mother didn't take steroids or any other medication for her rheumatoid arthritis. She began a regimen of vitamins and herbs, exercising daily, and freeing her spirit from anything that had kept her bound. Please understand: my mom never discounted the importance of her physician;

however, she knew her healing and deliverance needed far more than just pain relief. She was able to take the doctor's wellness plan and work with it to eventually become pain free but more importantly to walk in forgiveness.

Watching my mom release the hidden emotions and feelings that she had carried for years helped me to allow the Lord to work in me through forgiveness. It did not happen overnight. I walked a three-year journey, not only finding myself but also finding the Creator who had made me unique, unlike anyone else. And now, this journey has enabled me to write this book, because I finally realized my solution.

In order to move forward, I had to understand forgiveness, the kind of forgiveness that my Father in heaven had given to me. I then realized that I could not accept His forgiveness until I began to forgive those who had done me wrong. I was even able to change my prayer for my ex-husband. Instead of asking the Lord to kill him with a train, I was able to pray for his salvation as I released him to the Father.

Wow! That was one of the most freeing statements I have ever made. We often do not realize we are walking in bitterness until that bitterness is replaced with forgiveness. There can never be genuine peace in our lives until we release all bitterness and unforgiveness.

STUCK ON PRIDE

As with disobedience and bitterness, pride can affect your whole life. Pride will rob you of the joy that can be given you by the Holy Spirit, and it is the sin that will keep you from crying out to God for forgiveness. Pride will cause you to view yourself through a distorted lens that disguises your shortcomings. While pride causes us to filter out the evil in ourselves, it also causes us to filter out God's goodness in others.

My mom showed me the fallacies of living with pride. She knew she loved God with her whole heart and had no desire to live unrighteously. Yet pride in her righteousness distorted her view of the need for forgiveness for her bitterness. It is so easy for a spiritually proud person to see the sins of others while neglecting their own.

When we allow pride to live in our hearts, we become far more concerned about others' perceptions of us than we are with the reality of the sin that is lurking inside. It becomes easy to get defensive as others challenge us. Like the religious Pharisees in the Bible, we point our fingers at everyone around us while stuffing our secrets further and further down. Pride will blind us from the truth, and we will begin to live a lie.

Our weapons are not carnal but mighty in God for pulling down strongholds—pride is one of those strongholds! Our greatest weapon against pride can be found in prayer and God's Word.

> We use God's mighty weapons, not worldly weapons, to knock down the strongholds of human reasoning and to destroy false arguments. We destroy every proud obstacle that keeps people from knowing God. We capture their rebellious thoughts and teach them to obey Christ. (2 Corinthians 10:4–5)

Pride goes before a fall (Proverbs 16:18). When we believe our sins are greater than His grace, we are allowing pride to rule. If this God who created the universe and holds us in His hands could totally turn our lives from darkness into light, can we not respond to His presence and allow Him to cleanse us of our sins?

Let me repeat, pride goes before a fall. It can be so subtle that you think you are walking in humility, and yet you become proud of your humility. Isn't that wild?

Isn't it amazing that pride hungers for attention and respect? Have you known people who can never say no? They will complain about exhaustion while feverishly doing whatever is asked of them. Maybe they just can't say no, or maybe they need to feel needed. Maybe they are so desperate for the attention of others that they are afraid to decline because they cannot handle being alone. They are afraid you will no longer want them in your tribe.

I think more of us struggle with pride than we realize. Thankfully, there is good news for the prideful. When you confess that you struggle with pride, it signals the beginning of the end of the spirit of pride. Just as your concealed pride moves you through sin to death, acknowledging there is a problem with pride causes you to cling to the righteousness of God in Christ:

> Search me, O God, and know my heart;
>   test me and know my anxious thoughts.
> Point out anything in me that offends you,
>   and lead me along the path of everlasting life.
>
> (PSALM 139:23–24)

We open ourselves up to humility when we ask God to look inside the core of our being and pull out anything that corrupts our spirit. Anything that causes us to even think we can be successful without Him must go!

STUCK ON IMAGE

We all care what others think about us. But for some of us, it permeates every facet of our lives even when we may be unaware of it. Caring about what others think can become a full-time job as we become obsessed with our appearance, life choices, or even our daily conversations. Because my ministry involves social media platforms, I can tell you that these platforms only magnify the need for approval as we upload personal photos and give descriptive accounts of our lives. Throughout the day, I minister to small thumbnail photos of followers who have become like family to me as I assist them in navigating life's challenges. While seeking approval from others may be inevitable, it's so easy to forget that God made each of us one of a kind:

> You made all the delicate, inner parts of my body
> and knit me together in my
> mother's womb.
> Thank you for making me so wonderfully
> complex!
> Your workmanship is marvelous—how
> well I know it.
>
> (PSALM 139:13–14)

When we allow another person to determine our feelings about ourselves, we have allowed them to become an idol. If you find yourself seeking the approval of others, maybe it's time for you to turn your eyes upon Jesus and remember you are wonderfully and beautifully made.

God never took time to make a nobody. He made everybody special. You should no longer allow yourself to be stuck on your physical image and what others judge you to be. No longer will you be stuck on image.

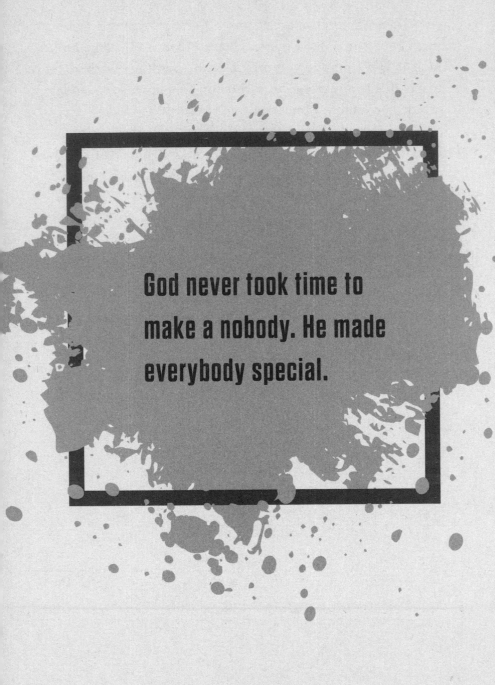

God never took time to make a nobody. He made everybody special.

GETTING UP!

DECLARATION

I once thought I was broken beyond repair. Now I know I am the apple of God's eye and He knows my name. I am fearfully and wonderfully made. I release every negative thought that has kept me imprisoned in my stuckness. I release every petty, disobedient, bitter, and prideful thought that has tried to sabotage my life journey.

PRAYER

Jesus,
To know You is to love You. I want to understand the love You expressed when You went to the cross for me. I desire to be free from any judgment I have exhibited toward others, and I accept full responsibility for the pain I have caused. Help me become that one-of-a-kind vessel You had in mind when You formed me in my mother's womb.
Amen.

RADICAL RESTORATION

I found RTK about three o'clock one morning when I couldn't sleep. We were in the middle of lockdown at the start of the COVID-19 pandemic, and I was battling another restless night. I was fighting off a multitude of feelings and going through what seemed to be depression. Scrolling Facebook, I came across one of Bishop Kim's replays. I immediately felt a spark in my spirit.

A few days later, I joined the Inner Circle family and became involved in the chats, devotionals, and Facebook sessions. Slowly, I started coming back alive in my spirit. Little did I know, a few months later I would encounter one of the biggest tests of my faith. God was already preparing me for that road by sending

Bishop Kim and the Inner Circle to my life. He knew I needed the wisdom, guidance, and bluntness Bishop Kim would be able to give me.

Through her ministry and the support of the IC family, I have been able to come out of my wilderness season and am walking in the freedoms and blessings given to me by the Lord. Thank you, Bishop Kim! Thank you, IC family! We are a mighty force to be reckoned with, and I thank GOD for all of you!

—E

Chapter 3

YOU'RE NOT STUCK BECAUSE YOU'RE NOT A TREE

Many times, we are asking God to heal pain
and He's asking us to get up and leave it!
—RTK

How often do we allow a season to define our whole lifetime? I am thinking about the man at the pool of Bethesda who, the Bible says, had been ill for thirty-eight years when Jesus came along one Sabbath:

> Afterward Jesus returned to Jerusalem for one of the Jewish holy days. Inside the city, near the Sheep Gate, was the pool of Bethesda, with five covered porches. Crowds of sick people—blind, lame, or paralyzed—lay on the porches. One of the men lying there had been sick for thirty-eight years. When Jesus saw him and knew he

had been ill for a long time, he asked him, "Would you like to get well?"

"I can't, sir," the sick man said, "for I have no one to put me into the pool when the water bubbles up. Someone else always gets there ahead of me."

Jesus told him, "Stand up, pick up your mat, and walk!"

Instantly, the man was healed! He rolled up his sleeping mat and began walking! (John 5:1–9)

I used to think that this no-named man had actually lain at the pool for thirty-eight years; however, the Bible only specifies the length of his illness, not how long he was at Bethesda. We have no idea how long he had been waiting at the pool for the chance to receive his healing. He is not called *lame*, yet he said he was unable to get himself to the pool. He must have been very weak and feeble with some type of disease that had stolen his ability to take care of himself. The Bible says he was unable to get to the pool without assistance, and no one had offered to help him.

There isn't an explanation of what sickness the man had; there was no doctor's diagnosis. The man was just described as sick. Could this have been emotional, physical, or even mental illness? Maybe the man found comfort in being with other broken people, so much so that he became more like them every day until thirty-eight years had passed. He had become stuck in a season.

Imagine this pool. It was a public bath, a five-sided hole in the ground filled with water where beggars with no social status gathered with those who came to use the bath. It was a common location for infirm people who were outcast from society. Interestingly, there were three types of people described in this story: the blind, the lame (physical inability), and the paralyzed. We see people who were broken from the inside out and those who were broken from the outside in.

The ancient Greeks had a cult for the ancient god of healing, named Asklepius, and during the Hellenistic period in Jerusalem, it was common for public baths to have healing sanctuaries. The Greek influence in the city meant that these pools were very popular among the ill and disabled. They were waiting to see when the water became troubled so they could receive their healing. This leads us to the word *egento*, which in the Greek means "overlooked."

A center for the overlooked. That is exactly the type of place where Jesus, God incarnate, wanted to "stir up" some people's lives.

The man had been in this condition for thirty-eight years. But then Jesus entered the scene and everything shifted.

I can so relate to this man. That's what Jesus did for me when I was at my lowest. I did not get to my lowest overnight; it took some time for me to reach that point. Was this man at his lowest? When we meet him, he was among a bunch of beggars at a public bath where he was unable to get into the pool on his own.

Can you imagine how the man felt when Jesus told him to stand up, pick up his mat, and walk? Remember, he had been sick for thirty-eight years before this miracle. We're not sure how much this man could move and why he had stayed in this condition for so many years. It's hard to imagine that he could not find someone—anyone—to help him reach the pool, yet he remained stuck until Jesus intervened. This man lay in the midst of many who had also been stuck for so long and could not figure a way out. I think that many of us would be trying to rationalize this situation. *Why me? Why just me? Why not the entire crowd that was waiting here? Who is this man who told me to get up?* Yet, once he encountered Jesus he instantly got up, rolled up his mat, and began walking.

How long have you been in your condition?

This man had become stuck in his condition. He had allowed his condition to dictate his season. He did this so long that his season became a lifetime. But when Jesus came by, this man was ready for change. You cannot move out of your low season and move on to your next stage in life until your desire for something new becomes greater than your desire to hold onto the familiar past.

———

I'm a lover of good brewed coffee, the kind of coffee that starts with the best coffee beans, freshly ground and then roasted to perfection. Don't give me a cup of instant coffee. There is no comparison between a coffee specially prepared and that teaspoon of instant gratification. I will wait in a long line to get the best, no matter how much time it takes.

The same goes for your deliverance. When you truly want to get unstuck, you won't care how long it takes or what the process looks like. In my process of getting unstuck, I wanted instant gratification while releasing layer after layer of mental and physical pain. "Jesus, You hold all things together. Why can't You just rush the process and do it quickly?" was my prayer.

The water in the pool brought healing to those who made it into the pool. But that water was an impersonal object, a channel that allowed Jesus to perform a personal act. The command Jesus gave the man to pick up his mat had a purpose. The mat had become the man's identity, a symbol of his defeat. Jesus told him to pick up his mat and clean up his area because he was not coming back. But he first had to get up! What Jesus did then and still does today is establish a new functioning identity for those who are stuck.

This man did not even know Jesus' name—the One who had raised him up—yet he obeyed and found his freedom. I wonder how many times we refuse to move because we will not simply face the fear and do it anyway? What did this man have to lose? He had been helpless and hopeless for years, so why not give Jesus a chance? This man did, and it worked! When you submit yourself to Jesus to get unstuck, you will triumphantly walk in freedom when you are healed.

The reason the man by the pool had to carry the mat was because people associated him with the mat. Jesus was telling him to clean up his room so he would not be comfortable going back to that place of brokenness. When we hand our brokenness over to God, He wants us to walk in freedom as we are released from the burdens of addictions and pain that have dictated our stuckness. The mat that was once the man's sign of defeat was now a sign of redemption. Just like our example, Jesus Christ. He carried the cross to Golgotha, which was a sign of defeat, yet He was moving toward redemption. He was about to set the whole world free from sin.

Do you think all the man's friends or acquaintances at the pool of Bethesda wondered what he had done to deserve his miracle? Many times we meet people who applaud us for where we are in our journey, especially when we are succeeding. They want us to speak or sing or bring life in our own way in this season. That's all well and good, but where were they when we were going through our breakdowns and our isolation season?

It's easy for people to ride with you as long as you have gas in your car, but where are they when the gas runs out? They didn't see when you were alone and felt like you couldn't make it through another day. What they see is the anointing upon you today because you were crushed and you allowed the crushing to produce oil yesterday. Many of the people walking with you in your miracle season probably did not see the price you paid to obtain your healing and deliverance.

Many times I felt like throwing in the towel or just taking a break from the crushing. But during times like that, I would remember one of my dad's conference stories. My dad has always been my hero and seemed to have a solution to every problem that came up in our family. He was always taking care of not only our family but everyone else (it seemed) who had a need as well.

He was attending a conference with numerous speakers,

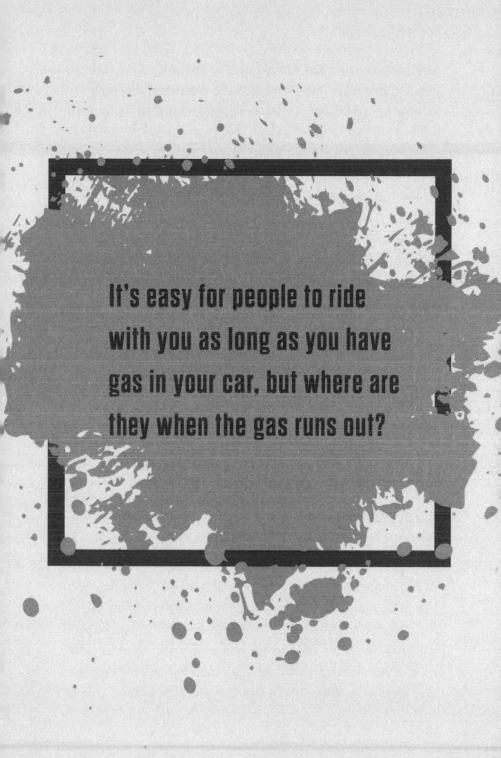

It's easy for people to ride with you as long as you have gas in your car, but where are they when the gas runs out?

prophesying over the attendees. He did not tell us that he needed a break from everyone who had been reaching out to him for assistance. Because this was his first conference with these particular speakers, my dad was hesitant to hear what they would say. He knew he had been through a tough season in his ministry and needed a word of inspiration, so he became open to hear whatever God wanted him to hear. He had been in full-time ministry since age twenty and now he was in midlife and wondering if there was more to life than he was receiving. Today, we would call that place "midlife crisis." He told our family much later that he had even been considering opening a counseling center and leaving the pastorate to others.

After several prophets had given him inspiring words, a man from Africa stepped up and told the group that he had a word for my dad. He was not one of the speakers, yet this man spoke with such authority as he delivered his word. He said, "'If you throw in the towel, I will throw it back at you,' says God." Everyone was shocked at the simplicity yet directness of this word.

On the way home, my dad's friend asked him about the various prophetic words he had received. My dad told him that the most profound word came from the unknown African man. My dad would have gladly accepted a way out of his obligations, his ministry role, and his personal pain. We had no idea he was fighting such an internal battle.

My dad told his friend that he had been discouraged and had wondered how to get out of the season of fire that he was experiencing. The African man had assured my dad that God was with him in the fire and would take care of him. This had encouraged my dad more than any other prophetic words delivered that day.

I, too, have felt that I could not carry on and have considered "throwing in the towel" numerous times. In each situation, God assured me I was His own and that the anointing He had placed on my life was unlike any other. The trials and testing are what strengthened my trust in Him. I know He has my back.

There have been plenty of times I have withdrawn into the quietness to be infused with His anointing, knowing I would not make it through the darkness without His presence. In fact, my father taught me to "hush until I heal." It's easy for people to be attracted to the anointing they see on you in the public arena but not understand that each victory came at the high price of unseen darkness, aloneness, weariness, and exertion. We don't know the price of another person's oil, nor the pain it took to get it.

In the book of John, there are seven recorded miracles, among them the blind man who was told to go wash his eyes in the pool of Siloam and this man at the pool of Bethesda. One received new vision and the other received a new way to walk. These are great examples of getting unstuck. Jesus wants us to get a new perspective and to walk without baggage as we move into a new season.

Jesus went looking for the man from the pool of Bethesda and found him in the temple. Jesus told him to stop sinning or something even worse might happen to him. Oh my goodness! Could this man's thirty-eight years of misfortune have been caused by his lifestyle?

> But afterward Jesus found him in the Temple and told him, "Now you are well; so stop sinning, or something even worse may happen to you." (John 5:14)

What had the man allowed in his life that caused him to be broken for thirty-eight long years?

———

Now consider David, one of the greatest kings in the Bible. David's greatness was attributed to a combination of factors: courage, divine anointing, leadership skills, warrior exploits, and even his psalms. We read that David was a man after God's own heart.

> "But God removed Saul and replaced him with David, a man about whom God said, 'I have found David son of Jesse, a man after my own heart. He will do everything I want him to do.'" (Acts 13:22)

Remember that David was famous in his day. He was the shepherd boy who became king of Israel seventeen years after he was anointed for the role. David was a warrior and a worshipper, and eventually he stepped into the palace as king. Even though he carried the huge responsibility of leading the children of Israel, there came a day when David stayed home and sent his men into battle. This was the brave warrior who brought down Goliath, the giant, and who had the song written about him:

> "Saul has killed his thousands,
> and David his ten thousands."
>
> (1 SAMUEL 18:7)

Do you see the connection? Even David allowed himself to become stuck in a season of complacency. David stayed home from battle, saw Uriah's wife bathing, and sent for her. He allowed the spirit of lust to overtake him. An illicit affair followed while her husband was on the front line in the battle defending David's kingdom. David sinned.

Bathsheba, Uriah's wife, became pregnant and told David they were having a baby. Like most of us have done, David tried to cover up and hide his sins when he was caught. It's the Adamic nature in us that causes us to try to find a way out—we try to cover up our wrong decisions.

Look at Adam and Eve when they were in the garden of Eden (Genesis 3). God walked through the garden on a cool afternoon to have fellowship with His chosen two, the only human beings alive at that time, but He saw that Adam and Eve were trying to hide from Him. They had covered their naked bodies with fig leaves because for the first time they realized they were naked.

I am talking about a man and a woman who had the world at their fingertips. Their days were full of peace and tranquility in the most beautiful place on earth, yet they allowed Satan to manipulate them into sinning against God. When God asked why they were dressed and hiding, Adam gave excuses: "It's that woman you gave me. She offered me fruit from the tree of the knowledge of good and evil, and I tasted it. God, it's all her fault."

Then, Eve admitted that Satan had deceived her.

Remember, they had access to every tree in the garden except for the tree of the knowledge of good and evil. Adam chose to cast blame on Eve in an attempt to hide his own sin.

Now look at King David, the most famous warrior and king in the Old Testament. He sinned against God because he became complacent and decided to stay home instead of going into battle with his men. King David was in the lineage of Adam and Eve, and so are you and I. Like David, Adam, and Eve did, we can easily get stuck on stupid when we make excuses for our wrongs. You are never stuck in any season because you are not a tree! You can make the decision to take the next step to freedom. But you have to choose to get up!

> **We can easily get stuck on stupid when we make excuses for our wrongs.**

Trying to cover his sin, David sent word for Uriah to be brought home from battle. He thought for sure that Uriah would sleep with his wife and then David's sin would be hidden. However, this brave man was loyal to his king and his fellow warriors and refused to spend even one night in the comforts of his home. So, David again tried to cover up his sin by having Uriah killed at the front line.

Throughout my childhood I often heard my parents repeat these words to me: "Be sure your sins will find you out." David would have benefited from this advice! Soon, David moved Bathsheba into the palace, and she gave birth to David's son. The baby died as a result of David's sin. David received a similar message to the one Jesus spoke to that man at the pool of Bethesda, "Stop sinning or something even worse may happen to you." God's prophet Nathan visited David with an explicit word from God:

> I gave you your master's house and his wives and the kingdoms of Israel and Judah. And if that had not been enough, I would have given you much, much more. Why, then, have you despised the word of the LORD and done this horrible deed? For you have murdered Uriah the Hittite with the sword of the Ammonites and stolen his wife. . . .
>
> This is what the LORD says: Because of what you have done, I will cause your own household to rebel against you. I will give your wives to another man before your very eyes, and he will go to bed with them in public view. You did it secretly, but I will make this happen to you openly in the sight of all Israel. (2 Samuel 12:8–9, 11–12)

David received the message loud and clear, and he went on to live a life of repentance.

God has given us the freedom of choice, and we will be faced with choices every day. I have decided to follow Jesus and allow my decisions to be filtered through the Holy

Spirit. I will not allow my choices to keep me stuck in a difficult season when I have been called to greater exploits. As you continue reading this book, please decide to no longer allow your past poor decisions and circumstances to determine your season. It really does come down to the simple act of making the choice to get up. *You gotta get up!*

GETTING UP!

DECLARATION

I once thought that I could never move from my present situation. Now I know that I will not allow certain decisions to keep me stuck when I have the right to keep moving. I will pick up my mat and walk! I release every excuse I have allowed to keep me stuck in this season. I will no longer allow my past to dictate my present or my future. I have been made victorious so I will no longer live like a victim.

PRAYER

Jesus,
You have already paved the way to true freedom. Guide me through this journey to becoming free. Thank You for never giving up on me in the same way You never gave up on King David. Throw the towel back at me any time I try to throw it in and give up. Let me be an example of resilience because I can do all things in You.
Amen.

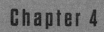

Chapter 4

STOP GIVING CPR TO DEAD SITUATIONS

Baggage is only baggage when you carry it.
Think about that. You have the power and
control to release it and move on.

—RTK

God is not a God of chaos and confusion. You keep RSVP-ing to the drama you've been invited to, so trouble keeps finding you. But miracles happen when you move. You can continually allow your past to dictate your present and your future, or you can determine it's a new season, a new day.

When you make that decision, you'll have to let go of those people and situations that helped facilitate your downfall.

You need to move some people from your VIP section of life to the balcony. Oh, you can still love them, just love them from a distance. Quit labeling yourself with the things you've gone through and what people have said about you. Just because you were divorced doesn't mean you have to call yourself a divorcée, or just because your spouse passes away, you don't have to label yourself a widow or widower, and just because you've lost your job, you don't have to label yourself unemployable. You don't have to allow others to label you either.

The prodigal son may have left home and returned broke and weary, but even though the world still labels him the prodigal, he was forgiven by his father and retained his position as a son. He had spent his entire inheritance, but his father made sure he was cared for the rest of his life.

Rahab may have been a prostitute when she protected the two spies sent by Joshua who were scoping out the land; however, when Joshua conquered Jericho, Rahab and her family were protected (Joshua 2; 6:23–24). Rahab eventually married Salmon and gave birth to Boaz, who later married Ruth. Even though this woman is in the lineage of Jesus Christ, people still label her "Rahab the harlot." She did not live out her label. She changed her situation and became a godly wife and mother.

God raised up a harlot to become the great-great-grandmother of King David. If you ask, "How could God possibly use a sinner like me?" I would introduce you to the woman who had been labeled a prostitute and was able to change her circumstances. She is not remembered for her sin but for the transformation of a family line from sinners to saints. The words *prodigal* and *prostitute* are undoubtedly repeated so that you and I will know that whatever we have done, God will forgive us as we come to Him in faith. People may have labeled us but we are covered by the blood of Jesus.

You are not what you've been through—that was only a season you walked through. But if you keep labeling yourself by the messes from your past, you will remain broken and trouble will keep returning again and again. You will be stuck in the same cycles for the rest of your life.

For a new season to break out in your life, you will need to make the decision to change and then to take a few steps:

- Decide
  Change occurs when you decide you will not live one more day imprisoned in your pain and you turn your life over to God.
- Define
  It is then important for you to define how and why you became entrapped so you can deal with the pain. Be honest with yourself and allow God to work in you. Remember, He is a gentleman and is waiting for your invitation.
- Detox
  Detox by renouncing any unclean spirit that has tried to attach itself to you through people, places, and things. Often we allow outside influences into our lives without even realizing it. Spiritual toxins can be taken in by scrolling on social media, through stressful environments, gossip, actions that we allow, decisions that determine our altitude, and so forth. Just like we can detox physically, it's possible to detox spiritually. Focus on your values and begin living an authentic

life, which means being true to who you were created to be. Get rid of the clutter or junk in your life in order to make room for a simplified version of you. Love yourself and begin to see that you were created specifically for this time and season. This will set you free to begin a new walk with God.

- Delete
  After detoxing, repent of the life you have lived and the wrong decisions that caused you to become broken. Let go of those things that have caused you distress and allow the process of elimination to become your friend.
- Discipline
  Discipline creates habits, habits become routines, and routines become who you are consistently. When you live a disciplined life, you will make small sacrifices in the present to create a more peaceful life in your future. Permanent results sometimes come with temporary discomfort.

This sounds so simple, doesn't it? It is, if you no longer allow brokenness from the past to inhabit your present. Choose to close all doors you have opened that allowed havoc into your life and into the lives of those you love. Closing doors means ending all access points, opportunities, and gates that the enemy could use to reenter your life. This may include relationships, associations, environments, deliberate breakups, and unforgiveness. You need to make sure certain people understand the relationship is over. Let them know you are now on a different path of life with Jesus.

One of the hardest decisions for me was becoming

disciplined as a true follower of Jesus Christ. It's one thing to declare you are a Christian and another thing to live a life that is an example of the Christian faith. To be like Jesus means you have no problem saying that you are sorry when you have failed others. That was a big deal for me when I began my new walk with Jesus Christ at the age of thirty-six.

I cannot blame my bad decisions on my family. I had been raised in a pastor's home, and my parents lived true Christian lives. I really had no excuse for being so immature at such a mature age. I just did not like anyone telling me how to live, so I chose to live my life unlike anyone else in my family. My ex was also from a pastor's home, so we had no excuses for the life we chose together. I am so thankful that God gave me chance after chance to put my life in order after I failed Him so many times. I, to this day, am amazed at how He always came through for me right on time.

I think about the three years of healing and deliverance it took me to totally surrender and allow God to be Lord of every aspect of my life. Did it have to take three years? Absolutely not! I was one stubborn girl who refused to allow anyone to dictate her life decisions. Even today, I cannot tell you the reason I would not allow anyone to instruct me in the ways of the Lord. I question myself as to why I could not simply ask God for forgiveness and then forgive myself for all the things I had allowed. I think about the apostle Paul and his journey. He made some profound statements that brought me deep solace during times of distress:

> I want to do what is good, but I don't. I don't want to do what is wrong, but I do it anyway. (Romans 7:19)

If this prolific writer—trained in the best of schools, a member of the Sanhedrin court, and even in the lineage of Benjamin—had a problem controlling his flesh, it gave me solace that God would be with me, too, as I made my journey of self-denial. After reading about Paul's life, I realized that everyone who has ever walked on this earth, except Jesus Christ, has one thing in common: we have all messed up.

It's up to us, however, to determine that we are sick and tired of the mess and want positive change to affect every area of our lives. Under the fake smiles, the made-up exterior, and the Christian lingo, we are on the same playing field. We mess up, get up, start over, try again, then mess up again. But the key is to get back up! Failure is not failure unless you stop moving.

Failure is not failure unless you stop moving.

I know everyone doesn't struggle with alcohol, drugs, promiscuity, or gambling, but we all struggle with sin in some form. When Paul said that every time he wanted to do good, he did wrong, it gave me such peace. If Paul could finally figure this Christian walk out, then so could I. We all suffer from the "I can't help its."

I know that God has a preordained plan for those who choose Him. One of my favorite scriptures will always be Jeremiah 1:5:

> "I knew you before I formed you in your
>   mother's womb.
> Before you were born I set you apart
>   and appointed you as my prophet to the nations."

I can't even explain how much this scripture ministered to my spirit as I was reflecting on my past and wondering how God could ever want to use a stubborn, rebellious girl like me. He assured me again and again that He loved me despite me.

———

Like a lot of us, Jacob's claim to fame was that he messed up (Genesis 32). He swindled his brother, tricked his father into giving him the birthright of the firstborn, and ran away to save his own life. Who could believe that God would choose him for anything except judgment? We see many times in the Bible, however, that God can take misfits and turn them into brave warriors. I am so thankful that God doesn't only use the brilliant, the most studious, the beautiful or handsome. He also takes the misfits, the down-and-outers, the failures, and sets them up to become mighty orators, pastors, counselors, prayer warriors, and teachers in the kingdom of God.

God sees you on the other side of your situation and sets you up for your next appointment. Next time you run into one of your haters full of judgment, just tell them that they may only see your failure, but God knows your potential. I can tell you this because I have experienced the failures, the backbiters, the judgments, and now live in a sea of forgiveness. Jesus gave me chance after chance after chance until I finally accepted that He was not going to give up on me.

I waited patiently for the LORD to help me,
and he turned to me and heard my cry.

He lifted me out of the pit of despair,
    out of the mud and the mire.
He set my feet on solid ground
    and steadied me as I walked along.
He has given me a new song to sing,
    a hymn of praise to our God.
Many will see what he has done and be
    amazed.
They will put their trust in the LORD.

(PSALM 40:1–3)

David knew that God had predestined his outcome. Remember, David was a misfit himself who had made some errors in judgment and sinned, yet he went to God in repentance and God forgave him. As I read about David's life, I realized that if God could say that David was a man after His heart (Acts 13:22), God could see my deepest thoughts and would help me as He did David.

God helped me out of the deepest, darkest pain I had allowed to erupt as my marriage ended. I realized during that time that the deepest desire my sons had—to grow up in an intact family—was null and void. Their parents were too broken to give them the one thing that meant everything to them. Maybe it was because I still thought I could control my world that it took me so long to finally give up my will, release the pain, and begin a new life as a single woman with two boys.

Sitting outdoors at a restaurant recently with my sons and my mom on my youngest's birthday, the desires of family came up in our conversation. My boys are so sentimental about holidays and family gatherings. I feel their pain as they replay their papa's (my dad's) journey with dementia and how much they miss him since his death. He was the father figure in their lives after the divorce. I realize I am unable to reestablish the family unit they so desired, yet they are still focused on living their best lives with their mom and Mimi (my mom). It took me years to finally determine I needed to close the door on my marriage, but I realize now that the reason I waited so very long is because I knew my boys needed to see that I had tried.

After three years, my mother accompanied me to visit the divorce attorney as I wept and told him my story. Without hesitating, he explained that I had endured emotional abuse and would need abuse counseling before divorce. As I began this journey, it set me up to deal with issues that had been locked up tightly in my memory bank but were now ready to be healed.

FINALLY, DELIVERANCE

I sought out a minister friend who could take me through the deliverance process of letting go of hidden hurts. I encourage you to find a safe person, someone appropriate to your situation, to help you on your journey.

Some of the most important advice I can offer you is to allow yourself to release anything that has caused you pain and to allow healing to take place in your spirit, will, and emotions. I often think about my decision to let go and realize that I was unable to do it alone. The Holy Spirit became real to me during those nights in my bed upstairs at my parents' home. He assisted me in forgiving those whom I had allowed to control and manipulate me.

———

After my boys and I moved out of our home and moved in with my parents, their father would come to visit on birthdays and Christmas. He would stay overnight, and before long he had moved into my bedroom.

This lasted six months. I worked while he stayed at home playing on the computer all day long. I finally realized that nothing had changed in our marriage except location. We were still in the same dead-end relationship; I was working, and he was playing. Finally, one day I came home from work as he was packing luggage to travel to his parents' home for a funeral. The problem was, he was not carrying an overnight bag. He had a large piece of luggage stuffed full of clothes. When I asked why he was carrying so many clothes for an overnight trip, he told me he might need them while he was gone.

This statement brought back memories of the last six years of our marriage when he would walk out of our house and be gone for several weeks or months. He struggled with drugs and alcohol and was driven by those addictions. I now see in retrospect how many holidays he missed. When he returned home after a holiday, he would want to decorate our yard with Halloween or Christmas decorations even though the holiday had already passed. It was as though this special family event did not matter to him until he was ready to celebrate in his own time. It was an embarrassment to our boys because they knew the neighbors would be talking about their broken family. Better to keep the pain hidden within the walls of our gorgeous home so they could pretend it wasn't even happening.

Not only was he broken, but I was also broken. We were in a codependent relationship, and it was like a merry-go-round at the carnival. There was no way to get off and take a break unless the entire system shut down. It was up to me to make the decision to no longer allow the dysfunction to rule our family.

This girl had been so full of pride that I had never allowed anyone to know how bad the situation had become. When my parents called, they didn't know that my ex wasn't at home. One reason I spend so much time with my mom these days is because we missed making memories during my tumultuous marriage. My parents included my boys in all the family vacations—to the mountains, to Hawaii, to Disney—but I was never in the family photos because I was at home trying to salvage a marriage I hoped was worth saving.

Remember, I had grown up in a pastor's home, so I knew what to do when the going got rough. When it seemed like there was no way out, I would listen to worship music and ask God for His assistance. When I reached that place where I knew there was nothing else that I could do, I turned to God. When my ex was absent for weeks, my little boys and I attended church as though we had never been gone. But when he returned, church was no longer in our schedule.

Honestly, it's amazing that today both my boys are in

church every Sunday morning. It is not because they were carried there by their parents while growing up. There was sadly no consistency of worship in a home where both parents had been raised to love and serve God. We had become two selfish people, and church was just not part of the equation. I'm telling you that I am a miracle in motion. When I made up my mind to get up and change, everything did change.

Look at the story of Jacob. Many would think it was over for Jacob when he ran away out of fear that his brother was going to kill him. Jacob had been so deceitful and manipulative:

> One day when Jacob was cooking some stew, Esau arrived home from the wilderness exhausted and hungry. Esau said to Jacob, "I'm starved! Give me some of that red stew!" (This is how Esau got his other name, Edom, which means "red.")
>
> "All right," Jacob replied, "but trade me your rights as the firstborn son."
>
> "Look, I'm dying of starvation!" said Esau. "What good is my birthright to me now?"
>
> But Jacob said, "First you must swear that your birthright is mine." So Esau swore an oath, thereby selling all his rights as the firstborn to his brother, Jacob.
>
> Then Jacob gave Esau some bread and lentil stew. Esau ate the meal, then got up and left. He showed contempt for his rights as the firstborn. (Genesis 25:29–34)

I'm not sure Esau realized how important the decision to give away his birthright was until his dad was preparing to die. When the time came for his dad to bless them, Jacob deceived his blind father into thinking he was Esau.

It's easy to understand Esau's position as the firstborn who was expecting to receive his inheritance as head of the family. He had forgotten that sunny afternoon when he was exhausted, weary, and needed a bowl of stew. He forgot that his brother had made him promise to give up his birthright, and anyway, it was up to their father to give the blessing. When Esau arrived that day to receive his blessing, his brother had already been there, deceived his father, and had been given the blessing of the birthright for the firstborn:

> Esau exclaimed, "No wonder his name is Jacob, for now he has cheated me twice. First he took my rights as the firstborn, and now he has stolen my blessing. Oh, haven't you saved even one blessing for me?"
>
> Isaac said to Esau, "I have made Jacob your master and have declared that all his brothers will be his servants. I have guaranteed him an abundance of grain and wine—what is left for me to give you, my son?" (Genesis 27:36–37)

Esau became enraged. I can understand why, can't you? Fearing for his life, Jacob ran. While Jacob was running away, he lay down in exhaustion and made a rock his pillow to get some rest. While sleeping, he saw a vision of a ladder coming down from heaven with angels ascending and descending. God was showing Jacob that He had provided around-the-clock protection for him.

When you read about Jacob's life, you see a young man who was always scheming and planning a way out. But God was always there protecting him from his own decisions. I realized that because I failed to allow God to be Lord throughout many seasons in my life, He would have to come along and rescue me again and again. As Jacob ran away from his brother, he ran into the arms of his uncle Laban. Years later, Jacob had matured but was still the undercover deceiver who ran away from his uncle and knew he would face consequences with his brother, Esau.

Even though God had assured Jacob that He would protect him, Jacob still reverted to his old scheming ways when it was time to meet Esau. But before Jacob could mess up one more time, God showed up while he was alone by the river Jabbock. Instead of resting and devising his next plan of action, Jacob wrestled with God. God knew that He would need to change Jacob. He would change his name from the old man called "the deceiver" to "Israel, the man who fought with God and man and won." God gave Jacob a permanent limp to remind him who God was, and then He gave Jacob a new name to remind him of what God is able to do.

"Your name will no longer be Jacob," the man told him. "From now on you will be called Israel, because you have fought with God and with men and have won."

"Please tell me your name," Jacob said.

"Why do you want to know my name?" the man replied. Then he blessed Jacob there.

Jacob named the place Peniel (which means "face of

God"), for he said, "I have seen God face to face, yet my
life has been spared." (Genesis 32:28–30)

Verse 30 says that God showed Jacob His face. When
Moses asked to see the face of God, God said Moses would
die if he saw His face. But, in this instance, God let Jacob
see His face so that he would no longer be concerned with
Esau or anyone else. No longer would Jacob need to practice
scheming or deception for protection. He finally had made
peace with his God and knew that God would take care
of him.

I lived thirty-six years trying to take care of me and
mine. I reached out to God only when there were no other
answers, and then God became a real presence to me. He
became the Lord of my life, and now I have an experience
with my God unlike anything else.

You cannot buy peace. There have been seasons when I
could not figure out the ending, yet I knew that God would
take care of me. I no longer bring relationships from my past
into my present unless God specifically instructs me to do
so. I no longer need to figure out my tomorrow because I
know that God has my tomorrow in His hands.

GETTING UP!

DECLARATION

I once thought I would never find the forgiveness that would allow me to change from my old self into a brand-new woman [man]. I will no longer give CPR to dead situations. I release everything that is not in alignment with God's assignment for my life. I am who God says I am! I release all the labels that were placed on me by myself and others. I choose to decide, define, detox, delete, and discipline for my next season.

PRAYER

Jesus,
You know all things. Teach me how to rest in that fact. Show me how to take my hands off things so that You can take over. I desire to be moved by Your words instead of my own emotions. Help me to be obedient even when it doesn't make sense.
Amen.

PART II
CHAOS SUCKS

When you move from crisis to crisis in your seasons of life, it gets messy.
You notice a general pattern in your moods. You move from restlessness to
negativity to unhappiness and then discontentment.

RADICAL RESTORATION

Since joining the RTK Inner Circle, I started listening to the *Real Talk Kim* podcast, which has changed my life. Every message is about something I am going through or have been through. In 2020, I got married out of desperation to someone I had known for only five months. I was thirty-eight years old and felt that my time was running out. Even though there were doubts, I went through with the marriage and immediately knew it was a mistake.

One night I listened to Pastor Kim's podcast episode "Stop Being Loyal to a Mistake." I knew she was talking to me. After much prayer and counseling from supportive Christian friends and the Inner Circle, I received the courage to file for divorce from my toxic marriage. Now I have a podcast and YouTube channel

and am publishing my first book. Being connected to Real Talk Kim and the Inner Circle brought me through one of the darkest seasons of my life, and I refused to stay stuck in a mistake any longer. I have never met a group like the Real Talk Kim Inner Circle nor anyone like Pastor Kim. There is so much genuine love and understanding. It's the closest thing to what I believe heaven will be.

—K

Chapter 5

QUICKSAND

I have survived too many storms to be concerned by a drop of rain.
—RTK

When you see life through a broken lens, every day looks like a crisis. You become codependent on deprivation and pain, to the point that, if it's not broken, you will eventually break it. You don't want to get healed because you have learned to live off the attention that being broken gets you. Peace and contentment are like a foreign language; chaos is your go-to. There may even be comfort in chaos.

Am I describing someone close to you . . . or, maybe, it's you?

The Oxford Dictionary describes *quicksand* as "loose wet sand that yields easily to pressure, sucks in anything resting on or falling into it, and a dangerous situation from which it is hard to escape." Do you ever have quicksand dreams in which you feel trapped and can't save yourself? This could suggest an internal battle you're fighting, or a relationship in which you have lost your way.

Let's look at Joseph, the man who stood side by side with Pharaoh, the ruler of Egypt. Joseph was not destined by inheritance or legacy to rule the nation of Egypt, yet that's where he was planted. No one would have imagined that Joseph, the young, favored son of his father, Jacob, would be forced to travel to Egypt and spend years away from his family. Joseph, when he was thrown into a pit by his brothers, must have felt like he was trapped in quicksand. He had no way of saving himself. The pit was too deep and there were too many brothers against him.

Isn't it amazing that Joseph's family, the very ones who had the same blood flowing through their veins, could turn on him and sell him for nearly nothing? It was all because of jealousy. Joseph was carrying a promise, but he did not have anyone around him who could assist him in following his dream. Is this why God allowed him to be sold to the Egyptian traders and taken to Potiphar's house? We know that God knows all things. He knows our going in and our coming out. He knows our beginnings and our endings, yet He has given us free will to choose our destination.

> O Lord, you have examined my heart
>   and know everything about me.
> You know when I sit down or stand up.
>   You know my thoughts even when I'm
>   far away.

You see me when I travel
and when I rest at home.
You know everything I do.
You know what I am going to say
even before I say it, LORD.
You go before me and follow me.
You place your hand of blessing on
my head.

(PSALM 139:1–5)

God's knowledge of our physical world does not limit His intimate knowledge of us. He knows what our conversations will be long before we even begin them. He knew Joseph would be sold into slavery, jailed after being falsely accused, only to become second-in-command to Pharaoh over the nation of Egypt. Just because Joseph met betrayal, rejection, and persecution, God did not negate his purpose and destiny.

One night Joseph had a dream, and when he told his brothers about it, they hated him more than ever. "Listen to this dream," he said. "We were out in the field, tying up bundles of grain. Suddenly my bundle stood up, and your bundles all gathered around and bowed low before mine!"

His brothers responded, "So you think you will be our king, do you? Do you actually think you will reign over us?" And they hated him all the more because of his dreams and the way he talked about them.

Soon Joseph had another dream, and again he told his brothers about it. "Listen, I have had another dream," he said. "The sun, moon, and eleven stars bowed low before me!"

This time he told the dream to his father as well as to his brothers, but his father scolded him. "What kind of dream is that?" he asked. "Will your mother and I and your brothers actually come and bow to the ground before you?" But while his brothers were jealous of Joseph, his father wondered what the dreams meant. (Genesis 37:5–11)

Joseph's promise was wrapped up in a haughty young man who had specific dreams of grandeur. I'm talking about Joseph himself. There was no one connected to him who believed in his dreams. Even his father listened but did not support him. His father scolded him for dreaming such an outlandish dream! I'm sure his father was wondering why Joseph was dreaming such expansive dreams about things he had never experienced. We see that his brothers became jealous, not only because he was a dreamer but also because they knew Joseph was their father's favorite son. So, when he was thrown into the pit by his brothers, it launched him into a season of quicksand.

Joseph was just beginning a crisis that would last for many years. He had no idea if he would ever see his father again. He knew his brothers hated him and meant to destroy him. Such fear must have engulfed this young boy as he was in the darkness of the pit! How could his brothers have had so much hatred toward him that they would dip his multicolored, one-of-a-kind coat in blood to make his father believe that an animal had killed him? Then the Egyptian traders came along, and his brothers sold him. The favored child was now being taken to Egypt as a slave.

I cannot begin to imagine the emotions that Joseph was processing as he was dragged along with the other slaves. He had lost the coat of many colors his father had given him as a symbol of his position in the family. His security had been stripped from him, and he had no one to protect him or stand up for him. I doubt Joseph imagined there was a purpose for his pain and his mistreatment.

When Joseph arrived in Egypt, he was carried to the market to be sold as a slave to Potiphar, the captain of Pharaoh's guard who was responsible for protecting Pharaoh's life. Joseph might have been sold as a slave by his brothers; however, he was still the same young man chosen by God for more than he could have imagined.

> The Lord was with Joseph, so he succeeded in everything he did as he served in the home of his Egyptian master. (Genesis 39:2)

Potiphar grew to like Joseph. The more he delegated to Joseph, the more the Lord blessed Joseph and, in turn, Potiphar. Joseph became Potiphar's administrative assistant in full charge of every aspect of Potiphar's enterprises. Joseph was also instructed to leave Potiphar's wife alone, which was no problem for Joseph since he was a man of character.

> And Potiphar's wife soon began to look at him lustfully. "Come and sleep with me," she demanded.
> But Joseph refused. "Look," he told her, "my master

trusts me with everything in his entire household. No one here has more authority than I do. He has held back nothing from me except you, because you are his wife. How could I do such a wicked thing? It would be a great sin against God." (Genesis 39:7–9)

Up until this fateful day, everyone respected Joseph. He gave no reason for anyone to distrust him. Joseph knew that he had to get away from this woman as quickly as possible:

She came and grabbed him by his cloak, demanding, "Come on, sleep with me!" Joseph tore himself away, but he left his cloak in her hand as he ran from the house. (Genesis 39:12)

It's as though Joseph hit another season of quicksand just as things had started to settle down. With his cloak in her hand, Potiphar's wife lied about Joseph, used his cloak to try to prove his guilt, and accused him of trying to seduce her. Potiphar, believing that his wife was telling the truth about Joseph, had Joseph thrown into prison.

How many times have you found yourself locked up in situations that were not your choice or your fault? You can probably relate to this man of reputable character who did nothing to deserve what happened to him. Joseph's truth did not matter to Potiphar, even though he stood only for what was right.

As a prisoner in a foreign country, Joseph could not contact family members to assist in his release. He had no one but God on his side. But God did not abandon him. In prison, Joseph found favor with the warden who put him in charge of the entire prison, and he was responsible for everything that happened there.

Do you understand the importance of having a true relationship with God? It does not matter whether you are sold as a slave and lied about by those whom you expect to stand by you; God will work in each situation and bring you out of the quicksand of life.

> And we know that God causes everything to work together for the good of those who love God and are called according to his purpose for them. (Romans 8:28)

Have you wondered what Joseph did when he was not taking care of prison activities? If the walls in his jail cell could talk, what would we learn about Joseph's musings? Think about those times when you have come to the end of any semblance of normalcy. You make one decision and it's as though everything in life has been created to punish you for being born. You go from one failed marriage to the next, coupled with financial failure and then, of all things, you become sick and unable to work. It's as though you will never see another happy season. Yes, I'm sure Joseph had those moments. He was an earthly man, like us, and he faced the same types of trials, rejection, betrayal, lies, and so forth.

Joseph built the kind of foundation described in Proverbs 24:3–4. He built it throughout many seasons of deceit; the deceit not by Joseph but by everyone connected to him. Joseph chose to continue to do what was right even when he was treated unfairly. He made wise decisions instead of being ruled by emotions.

> A house is built by wisdom
>   and becomes strong through good sense.
> Through knowledge its rooms are filled
>   with all sorts of precious riches and valuables.
>
> (PROVERBS 24:3–4)

If your walls could talk, what would the world know about you? Would they speak of your faithfulness in your marital relationship? Would they say that you support your spouse and your children? Would they testify that Jesus is Lord of your life and that you bring strength into your home? Or would they hear that you are quarrelsome and fail to maintain peace in your relationships?

If your walls could talk, what would the world know about you?

I believe that Joseph was an amazing example of peace in the midst of the storm. There is no way that he succeeded without knowing how to praise his way through challenges. Throughout Joseph's life, he never lost sight of the One who was in control. He may have become discouraged when he was forgotten by those he needed most while in prison, yet he still maintained character in the middle of his trial.

It's easy to lose sight of God's plans when you are in the middle of a storm. When times are hard and your world seems set against you, you can easily forget your dreams. How did Joseph manage his integrity when everyone believed he was guilty of the lies spread about him? The lie that he had seduced Potiphar's wife and deserved prison? Joseph had no idea that he would one day be second-in-command to Pharaoh in Egypt. Despite everything that came against him, he still maintained his belief in God.

Joseph could have allowed his dysfunctional family to become his excuse for failure. Locked up in prison, Joseph could have seen everything through the eyes of a prisoner. He could have placed blame on Potiphar or on Potiphar's wife and done foolish things to others. But what we see is Joseph serving others in prison. He did not allow his circumstances to determine his attitude. I'm sure Joseph heard many stories in prison from other prisoners who blamed their criminal acts and their jail time on the pain other people had caused. Yet through all of it, Joseph chose to keep his heart right.

Without a doubt, wounds from family cut deeply because family members are supposed to love and support one another. However, it is up to us to determine that we will allow forgiveness to overtake any kind of bitterness that would try to manifest itself in our lives. Locked up in prison and forgotten by all, Joseph could have focused on the bitterness he may have felt for his brothers who had sold him out. Instead, he spent each painful day trusting that God would bring him through the quicksand.

And if he had not served his masters as a loyal servant, he might never have seen the day when he would save not only his family but also millions of others during the greatest famine in Egypt's history. At the end of Joseph's story, his brothers needed help and because of his good character, he was the answer to their prayers.

———

Do you wonder why you have gone through rejection and betrayal? I can tell you that God has an earthly and a heavenly plan for your life. The world is filled with people who judge what they know nothing about and then attempt to educate people regarding what they have never experienced. It's easy for us to despise the painful seasons we've gone through, but God will use those seasons to help others if we allow Him.

Think about our example, Jesus Christ. What qualifies Jesus to help us? Our first response would be that He is the Son of God; however, the Bible tells us that Jesus *chose* to experience our pain:

> Even though Jesus was God's Son, he learned obedience from the things he suffered. In this way, God qualified him as a perfect High Priest, and he became the source of eternal salvation for all those who obey him. (Hebrews 5:8–9)

Jesus needed to experience suffering, rejection, and betrayal in order to be our High Priest so that He could truly understand the pain we would experience. He gladly took on suffering and abuse to walk in understanding as our Savior. Why can't we trust the process—that He is our Lord, He went to the cross, died, and rose again so that we can have abundant life? We now understand that the painful and unjust situations that happen to us do not come from God; however, He will sanctify them for His use. When you feel like you're in a quicksand season, you gotta get up! Remember that God's strong arm can pull you through!

GETTING UP!

DECLARATION

I used to think that I would never be released from my quicksand season. Now I know I am stepping out of the quicksand and walking into my God-given purpose. I am done being codependent on deprivation and pain. I release the dysfunction I allowed myself to get comfortable in. I will keep my heart right through any storm that comes my way and allow God to work it all together for my good.

PRAYER

Jesus,
To know You is to know perfect peace. I want to know how to hold on to Your peace during the hard seasons. Teach me how to keep my eyes on You, even when there is a storm going on around me. Help me to focus on what You are showing me in each season, just like Joseph, instead of becoming resentful.
Amen.

RADICAL RESTORATION

I grew up with a physically and mentally abusive father whom I did not realize until much later was my stepfather. My mom lived in survival mode after giving birth to me at age fourteen. When I was seventeen, after we were imprisoned for several hours, we escaped out a window in our pajamas on a rainy night.

I was dating the father of my children at that time. After eight years and two kids, we divorced, and he spent twenty years making my life hell in every way. During those years, I made the many mistakes a broken, lost person makes. I was struggling with depression and attempted unsuccessfully to end my life. . . .

It was during my third marriage with a cheating, narcissistic man that I found Pastor Kim, in 2017, and she spoke life into me. Over the years she led me into believing in myself, but I wasn't ready to forsake the sins of the world. I was still seeking love, affection, acceptance, and attention from a man.

I joined the Inner Circle in September 2021 and by January 2022 I knew I was ready for change and made plans to attend the RTK retreat. At that retreat I knew I was ready to die to my flesh and commit to a relationship with Jesus Christ. I have been on fire for God for an entire year and totally committed to a different way of life. My only interest now is to use my mess of a life to help others, whether those are children who went through what I did or women who need to find worth in themselves. I am no longer the victim. I am victorious. Pastor Kim guided me from who I thought I was to who God created me to be.

—C

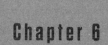

Chapter 6

UNDERSTAND THE PROCESS

When I was leaving my "quicksand season" and asking God to help me learn to love, I began feeling emotions in ways I had never felt before. The tears would just flow in that season, and I realized that to get to my destination of wholeness, I had to go through growing pains. No one had warned me about the pain that came with healing. In fact, if I had known the pain, I'm not sure I would have chosen the healing journey. It was real! But never underestimate the power of the process! The results of healing are well worth the journey.

> Never underestimate the power of the process!

In the midst of my pain, I realized I had options, and that was an important revelation. I could remain locked up in my prison of pain and allow hurt from the past to control each season of my life, or I could decide to get up and walk away from it. I could have allowed only broken people to influence my life because it's easy when people cosign on your dysfunction and pain. I can tell you that living without choice is no life at all. I now realize that my years of independent living while relying on no one to give me direction resulted in a season of loss.

How had I allowed deeply buried feelings to manipulate and control me to the point that I had no relationships or accountability? We all need restrictions and boundaries.

When we study Creation in the book of Genesis, we seem to focus on the content of what was being created each day and downplay the process. However, we know that God is a God of order, so there had to be order in the process. There were separations and divisions even in light and dark. There could be no day and night until darkness was exposed. Boundaries were established as the land and oceans were divided. God was showing His creation that boundaries had to be in place for life to thrive.

Both plant and animal life reproduce within boundaries according to their kind. Even the garden of Eden, which was the home of the first couple, Adam and Eve, had boundaries. There was a tree in the garden—the tree of the knowledge of good and evil—the fruit of which was not to be eaten. This God-given boundary demanded their trust in the Creator who formed them and placed them in their home. And yet, we know that Adam and Eve failed the test of boundaries when they ate the fruit from the tree and then were banished from the garden.

Guard your heart above all else,
for it determines the course of your life.

(PROVERBS 4:23)

It's a heart issue. Boundaries are basic guidelines we create to determine how others are able to behave around us. Until you have established healthy boundaries for yourself, you will be vulnerable to being used and abused by those whom you have allowed to enter your personal space. Setting boundaries ensures that your relationships are mutually respectful and caring.

We assume that people will respect our boundaries if we were taught to respect each other's space in our families. However, this is not the case in all relationships. It's easy to allow others to become possessive and controlling when boundaries are not in place. A power struggle will end with the most controlling one having the last word.

Too much power is dangerous, regardless of who possesses it. It's important to realize that we will have influencers in each season, and these influencers may change. Even though I lived for years *thinking* I was refusing others' influence, today I realize that I was actually being influenced by them. To take away choices is to remove your identity because the choices you make are a part of who you are. Maybe throughout those seasons, I had just wanted my voice to be heard.

I had suffered from insecurity since I was a child because of learning disabilities in school. As an adult who was broken, I had no idea how to become a balanced individual who allowed others to speak truth into my life. When there is lack of choice, there is a lack of uniqueness, of personality. I am so thankful that I can go to certain scriptures, like this one, that give me what I need as I walk this path of life today:

> We can make our plans,
>> but the LORD determines our steps.
>>>> (PROVERBS 16:9)

Solomon, the writer of this proverb, had asked God for wisdom, and he became the wisest king who ever lived. But he still failed God. His dad, King David, had encouraged him to walk with God with all his heart and soul. David did not instruct his son just to obey God but rather he instructed Solomon to walk with God. This piece of wisdom was one of the reasons I struggled for so long. I had no idea how to walk with God and allow those in authority to speak into my life. I refused to listen when I needed direction.

David's focus was on the success of his son's kingdom; he showed this by trying to encourage Solomon to develop a relationship with God. Solomon had been raised in a family that was devoted to the worship of the one true God, so it was assumed that Solomon would always be devoted to the God of Israel. He is known for being the king of Israel who built the temple in Jerusalem and was the last king of the unified Israel.

"Now, O LORD my God, you have made me king instead of my father, David, but I am like a little child who doesn't know his way around. And here I am in the midst of your own chosen people, a nation so great and numerous they cannot be counted! Give me an understanding heart so that I can govern your people well and know the difference between right and wrong. For who by himself is able to govern this great people of yours?" (1 Kings 3:7–9)

When Solomon became king of Israel, he sought after God, and God gave him the opportunity to request whatever he desired. Solomon asked for wisdom to govern God's people righteously. God not only gave him wisdom but also made him the wealthiest of all the kings who ever ruled:

"And I will also give you what you did not ask for—riches and fame! No other king in all the world will be compared to you for the rest of your life! And if you follow me and obey my decrees and my commands as your father, David, did, I will give you a long life." (1 Kings 3:13–14)

After becoming king, Solomon followed in the statutes of his father, David. But after some time, he formed a marriage alliance with the pharaoh of Egypt and took the pharaoh's daughter back to the city of David.

Solomon was breaking down the boundaries that had been established in Scripture for his protection. His marriage alliance led to hundreds of more alliances, and eventually, all these marriages turned his heart away from full allegiance to the God of Israel. All the wealth and abundance that looked like a sign of divine blessing for Solomon began to appear very different as he gradually sank into full compromise of the standards set up by his father. As you read

Solomon's life story, you will discover that all the kings of Israel after Solomon followed in his footsteps by forming unholy alliances.

Solomon was a man who had begun his reign with the intention of giving his all to God; nevertheless, his heart became insensitive to God's voice. His great wisdom that had once represented a gift from God became an instrument for his own exaltation and reward. Studying the life of Solomon revealed how I had allowed character flaws to erase boundaries that had been erected through my family lineage for my protection.

Solomon's life is a picture of a man created by God to do the will of God; however, he crossed boundaries, and the first chapter of Ecclesiastes contains a prime example of his end:

"Everything is meaningless," says the Teacher, "completely meaningless!" (v. 2)

Solomon had been revered by kings, countrymen, and even the Queen of Sheba, yet he wrote that everything is meaningless. He was telling us that our works in this life are temporary and will be forgotten. The only meaningful efforts are those we accomplish through the power of Jesus Christ.

My dad was a mover and a shaker. He traveled and ministered in churches as a sixteen-year-old. He would travel by bus to a city several hundred miles away, spend the weekend preaching, and take the bus home on Sunday night to attend school on Monday. When he married my mom at the age of twenty, he was already established as an evangelist who traveled throughout the southern states holding revival meetings. He would preach for hours and then pray for everyone who needed prayer. It was never about his health or strength. He just knew he wanted to make himself available to people if and when they needed him.

In one of his revivals as a twenty-four-year-old evangelist with a wife and child, after an exhausting service in which he preached and prayed for several hundred people, the pastor of the local church pulled my dad aside and warned him about being used up for the sake of the gospel of Christ. He told him that those people who lined up for healing every night of the revival would not even remember his name when he was worn out from ministry and passing on to his forever home.

The pastor said, "They will walk by your dead corpse and say, 'Doesn't Brother Jones look natural?' If they even remember your name."

My mom always reminded my dad of this when he was exhausted and would not take a break for even a few days of rest. Today my mom reminds me of this same thing because it's so easy to get caught up in the needs of the people. It can feel like there will be no breakthrough unless it comes through you, and it's hard to see that the important thing to remember is that it's all about Jesus Christ and Him being crucified for each one of us.

Our home was what you might expect a pastor's home to look like, especially decades ago. My dad was the head of our family, and my mom carried out his wishes. The more I study the Bible, the more I see the resemblance of my sweet mom in the image of Martha. She was always scurrying about, making sure everyone was taken care of, while learning Sunday's choir music for choir practice on Thursday. You see, the ideal pastor's wife in our world was musically inclined and able to instruct the women of the church while keeping our home spotless, just in case church members dropped by.

We were in a denomination that held very strict standards—no television, no sports, no jewelry, no makeup, and no pants for the women. The women were to be keepers of the home and were there to minister to their families. The only reason I even add this to my story is because, after many years of living this way, my dad began to realize that no matter how holy we tried to live, we could never be good enough, holy enough, or righteous enough to save ourselves. He realized that, in our self-righteousness, it became very easy to judge others when they were not meeting our standards of living for Jesus Christ. We had become professional judges of righteousness.

When my dad began receiving this insight, there was contention among those in the congregation who needed the pastor to instruct them on how to stay within our church's boundaries. At that time many of the families in our church did not want to seek God for direction when they had a pastor who could legislate righteousness for them. We'd become a church whose standards would indicate if a person had sinned.

For example, if women trimmed their hair or wore a wedding band, they had sinned.

Men's shortcomings or sins were normally not as public, such as watching television, so it was more difficult for theirs to be exposed. In fact, the only examples I can think of where men were exposed were when they were caught drinking in a bar or having an affair. This was one problem with our standards: women bore the brunt of the criticism when their sin was openly exposed.

It's almost comical how, even though the women were considered the weaker sex, it seemed they had to be the strongest when it came to living up to the standards.

As a teenager growing up in this type of environment, I watched as the choir sang until "they sang the glory down" on Sunday evenings. This was a service when everyone showed up and expected the choir to show out. I had a running conversation with myself as I watched the adults on Sunday evenings. The singing and music were rocking the house, but I wondered why the choir members didn't appear happy. I would think, *I certainly don't want to go to heaven with you guys. It would be miserable.* I felt like Solomon when he said life was meaningless. There had to be more to life than what I was experiencing.

My parents began their journey of understanding grace, and my dad, a student of the Bible, was studying commentaries and examining different Bible versions to obtain a clear understanding of what was right for us. My parents understood their decisions at that time would change us from that point forward. But as my parents moved toward grace, I moved toward discontentment and rebellion.

Watching families leave our church because they needed stronger standards or boundaries made me question the love of Christ. *Why in the world couldn't people serve God just because He had sent His only Son to die for their sins?* I didn't approach my parents with my questions because they were dealing with issues among the congregation and I was just a young girl trying to find my way. I had no idea that, just as Solomon left his father's covering by removing the old landmarks David had erected for his protection, I, too, was removing boundaries that had kept me safe within my family. My parents called them "standards of holiness."

As my parents' perspective shifted, their standards of holiness began to reflect their understanding of God's love and grace. No longer was I required to wear skirts and long sleeves. And when I was thirteen years old, my mother took me to a hair salon to have my hair cut for the first time.

My teenage self wanted the most audacious look possible. Does that surprise you? I doubt it! That haircut was the beginning of the many looks of Kimberly Jones. This opened the door for short sleeves, makeup, and jewelry.

My parents had no idea the struggle going on within my belief system, so they did what they did best. They loved me despite my decisions. Even when church leaders told my dad that he needed to restrict me, my dad would respectfully answer that I was his daughter, and he would always love me. And he did.

As I reminisce about my life before our change and my life after, I realize that I could never have become the strong woman I am today if my parents had not stood against the religious system at that time and determined it was time for something different. They loved those who criticized their choices, they forgave when forgiving was not the easiest, and they chose to hear God's voice as they made decisions for my brother, Rob, and myself.

I realize now that the next few years of my life were critical in assisting me in becoming the voice for the broken that I am today. Had I not made so many unwise choices throughout my journey, I'm not sure I could fully understand those who come to me feeling as though they have let the entire world down. Life is one process after the next. It might seem easy to say what decisions you would make if you are faced with a crisis such as a divorce or devastating illness. However, it's another thing when the choice is yours to make and that choice will dictate your legacy.

GETTING UP!

DECLARATION

I once thought that I was broken beyond repair. Now I know that I will always have choices to make. I choose to grow and glow through the process. I will no longer allow uncertainty and discomfort to dictate my progress. I know that the healing is worth every step it takes to get there. I release the control I thought I had, and I humble myself before the Lord.

PRAYER

Jesus,
Thank You for always having a bigger plan. You know what is in my past, my present, and my future. Help me to follow only Your voice as I choose to move forward.
Amen.

RADICAL RESTORATION

Real Talk Kim came across my Instagram feed one day with all her wild energy, and she had my attention. I was very cautious at first. The wild captivated me and scared me at the same time. I kept coming back.

God had used this girl to speak right through to the places that needed to be set free. She spoke bluntly with truth; she spoke directly with a humbleness of heart that draws you in. She spoke with authority that is contagious. She said to stand up in the midst of the battle and stand to win!

I am not the same person I was when I went through a betrayal after being married thirty-three years. A year later, the residue of pain had me stuck, but because of the obedience to the call, Kim (and, yes, she is so humble that we can call her Kim and there is no offense), in the midst of her own pain, made a choice to show up, speak up, and act me up for freedom from my past, freedom from the hurt, and freedom from the offense. I have been able to let the past go and be restored in a kingdom marriage that blesses me every day. This woman speaks the message of hope and healing that God gives her. She sets herself aside and serves with excellence and unconditional love the community that God has given her. Real Talk Kim is God's girl. I am now thirty-five years married, restored, and transformed because our words have power, and obedience changes lives.

—J

Chapter 7

STOP BLEEDING ON PEOPLE WHO DIDN'T CUT YOU

The pain you experience may not be your fault; however, the healing is your responsibility. It might be a long, complicated path to forgiveness. I can tell you through experience that getting to the point of forgiveness can be a hard journey. But freedom only comes after you can honestly say that you have truly forgiven the person who hurt you.

When I look back at some of the most painful moments of my life, I see myself sitting alone. I see myself feeling either immense shame or regret. It's so bizarre how we can become offended and angry yet repeatedly choose to torture ourselves far worse than others possibly could by rehashing the hurt in our minds over and over again.

For the longest time, my biggest regret was missing out on life. I did not begin ministry until I was forty years old. It

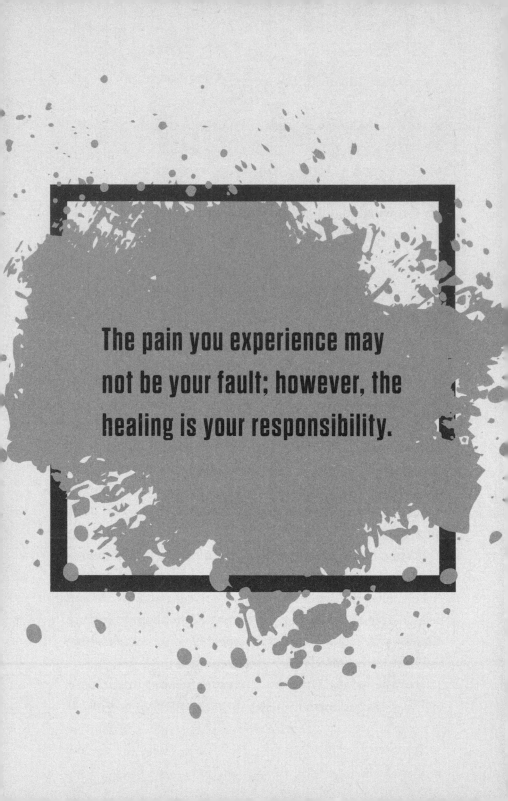

The pain you experience may not be your fault; however, the healing is your responsibility.

wasn't because I was preparing myself for a life dedicated to God, but because I had dismissed anything that would lead me to a life of fulfilled promises. During my healing journey, I missed out on family vacations. This was all because I had made so many errors in judgment. I was trying to recoup my losses.

Growing up, I lived in a home with parents who would have done anything to make me happy. I remember my dad driving me around the I-285 loop of Atlanta one night trying to persuade me not to get married. He promised a new car, college education from the best schools, and anything else he thought would appeal to me. His only daughter was preparing to begin a journey that was unlikely to end in happiness. However, my desire was to become an adult, get away from restrictions, and live life to its fullest. It's amazing how, in my immaturity, I thought life would be normal and exciting when living without restrictions.

From a distance, people probably thought I had everything going for me. But up close, you could see the cracks in the façade that I had built around my "idyllic" life. After marriage and having two gorgeous sons, I was painfully discontent, depressed, and often isolated in fear. I look back and am amazed at how God blessed me despite my rebellion.

My husband and I were both pastors' kids, but you would have thought from the way we lived that we had been raised in heathen homes with no thought of God. God was not first in our lives. Two very broken people were trying to make life look easy to anyone looking on.

It started for me at the age of six when my parents were

told that I had a learning disability and could not compre-
hend what I was reading. Why was I the misfit in my class?
How could my brother excel without even studying while
I could not grasp even the easiest phonics concept? I joke
today about the difficulty of reading my social media posts
because of this. I let everyone know that they may need
an interpreter when reading my posts because there are no
commas, only run-on sentences.

My mom and I rehearsed spelling words for the Friday
tests for hours and hours, only for me to fail because I could
not remember the words. During my adolescent years, I was
embarrassed and lacked self-confidence because I had been
labeled "learning disabled." I understand the challenges kids
face today with peer pressure and the stigma of social media
as everyone is trying to measure up. These life challenges
hardened me; it was a form of self-protection. I watched
my older brother win awards of excellence while I struggled
just to stay in school.

But I determined that what I lacked in education, I would
make up for in fortitude. My greatest passion is loving people
back to life, and I now dedicate my life to traveling the
world and spreading God's love to
everyone I meet. If you had told me

**My greatest passion
is loving people
back to life.**

then that I would be as active today
with podcasts, a YouTube channel,
and millions of followers on social
media, I would never have believed
it would be possible. It is still hard
for me to believe that I am an author of four books and am
sought after as a guest speaker for many events.

For years I regretted many of my decisions, and I could not move on because of paralyzing fear. I was always striving for more because I never believed I would be able to retain everything I had accumulated. I remember a certain time in my life when I carried with me a lockbox full of cash everywhere I went. Even when traveling out of state to visit my parents, I took my lockbox. It became a family joke. I trusted no one and believed that no one was capable of taking care of me the way I was taking care of me.

I lived in isolation because I did not know how to enjoy the present. From the outside, it looked as though I had everything—I had a gorgeous husband, two handsome sons, a fabulous home with a convertible sitting in the drive. My interior design business was successful and provided us with a life of luxury. Yet I knew we were living on the edge and all it would take was just a nudge to send us to ruin. God had given me everything I had desired, but I couldn't enjoy it because I lived in isolation with the fear that it would not last.

Now I can take my regrets, identify my weaknesses, and know that God has given me the strength to overpower anything that challenges me. I now understand that if I had not struggled, I would not have become this woman of force who now owns several businesses, pastors a bustling church, and travels fifty weeks yearly, speaking around the world.

The toxic relationships I forged kept me hostage until I came to the realization that I did not have to live with regrets for all the poor decisions I had made. What I did or didn't do could either paralyze me further or motivate me to do something new.

I remember the moment I came to the decision that it was time for me to take my life back; regrets would not keep me in isolation any longer. My situation had not changed, but I had found the endurance needed to break free of the guilt and shame. I had to deal with the why of being so afraid to believe in myself. It was time for detox—time for me to change the people and change the playground that had become my favorite place.

LET GO OF REGRETS

Everyone makes mistakes. Until we fully grasp this concept, we will continue going through life looking for change but finding none. It's time to let go of your regrets.

Use your mistakes as a teaching tool. You can bounce back and not repeat cycles—I've seen people do it over and over. When I became transparent and began taking the world with me on my daily journey, it changed me. I no longer had skeletons in my closet nor was I afraid to reach out to others. People knew my story and still loved me.

I no longer live in fear of someone knowing my secrets. I have no secrets to hide. I am no longer embarrassed that I am a divorced mother of two. It's time for you to stop worrying about what others think about you. Instead, use your failures and mistakes to help others. When you realize that what you are going through may make a difference for others, it changes you. God trusted you with your mess so you can impact others with His message.

I stopped allowing others to control my days when I

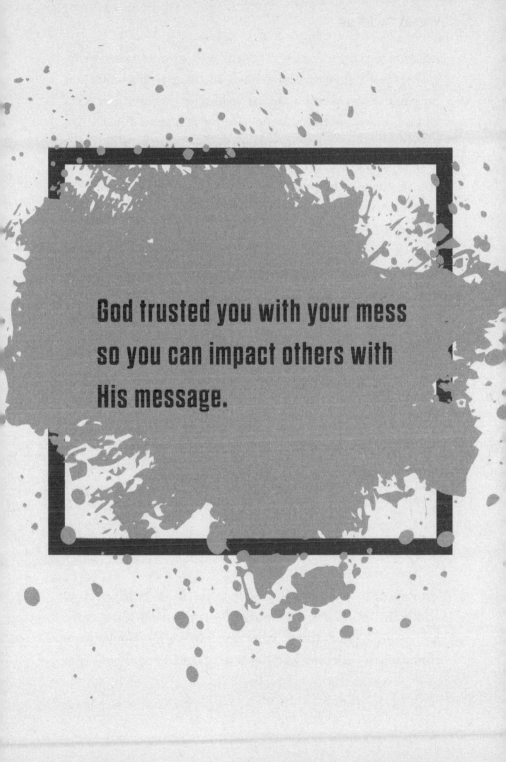

God trusted you with your mess so you can impact others with His message.

began facing my regrets and mistakes. It's time to stop being embarrassed that you have been in drug rehab or in jail. Stop allowing others' opinions to determine your direction when God wants to use your pain for His gain. You will be amazed at how many people you could impact if you get honest and tell the truth about your mistakes. Don't let your failures go to waste!

Everyone who has heard my story knows that I have determined to tell it like it is. I got married for the first time at eighteen, and it is just a blur in my memory book. My mom has joked that the wedding lasted longer than the marriage. I truly don't even remember the time we were together. I have used that mistake to help so many people on their journeys.

I married again without listening to wise counsel because I thought I knew what was best for my life. Boy, was I wrong! Out of that marriage came my two gorgeous sons and many years of painful memories. I could have spent my entire life bleeding on people who did not cut me, but I finally realized at age thirty-six that I must take responsibility for the pain I had inflicted and for the decisions I had made.

The apostle Peter was a prime example of failure. How could this man who had walked with Jesus—Jesus, who had even healed his mother-in-law—deny Jesus three times when everyone had deserted Him? Peter knew that

Jesus was going to be crucified and had promised Jesus that he would never forsake Him. But at the most crucial time in history, Peter's fear drove him to fail the One he called friend. In the garden of Gethsemane, Jesus warned Peter to stay awake and pray because the spirit might be willing but the body was weak. Peter fell asleep and, by the time the soldiers had come to arrest Jesus, it was too late to pray for the strength to endure.

Peter learned his lesson about being watchful. Peter assumed that he was strong enough to withstand any temptation as he stood with Jesus. He failed to realize that we can let our emotions overpower us even when we have set our goals to be strong in the Lord. But his enemy had targeted Peter because he had not prepared himself through prayer, and he underestimated his weakness.

> Stay alert! Watch out for your great enemy, the devil. He prowls around like a roaring lion, looking for someone to devour. (1 Peter 5:8)

Peter came to himself as soon as he heard the rooster crow and realized that he had denied his Lord three times just as Jesus had prophesied. Peter mentioned that our enemy prowls like a roaring lion, waiting for someone to devour, which means that he is always waiting. The devil is patient and can wait until we let our guard down. Why did Jesus allow Peter to fail so miserably? Jesus revealed to Peter that Satan had asked for permission to sift the disciples like wheat:

"Simon, Simon, Satan has asked to sift each of you like wheat. But I have pleaded in prayer for you, Simon, that your faith should not fail. So when you have repented and turned to me again, strengthen your brothers." (Luke 22:31–32)

Jesus could have protected Peter, but Jesus had a higher goal. He needed to arm Peter in the fight to strengthen the other disciples. Peter was equipped and able to rise up as a leader in the early church, teaching and training others to follow the Lord Jesus Christ. He was the special speaker on the day of Pentecost when the Holy Spirit was poured out on the 120 people in the upper room in Jerusalem and spoke to thousands during the Passover celebration. As He does with our failures, God used Peter's failures to turn him from Simon, a common man with a common name, into Peter, whose name means "the rock."

HOW DO YOU VIEW YOURSELF?

How do you view yourself? It's an important question to answer if you are ready for change. If you do not answer this question biblically, you will never be able to find the peace you've been searching for:

But you are not like that, for you are a chosen people. You are royal priests, a holy nation, God's very own possession. As a result, you can show others the goodness of God, for

he called you out of the darkness into his wonderful light.
(1 Peter 2:9)

I see five descriptions of who we are in this verse. Understanding who you are will help you as you express your faith to others. Peter would never have understood his worth if it were not for his shortcomings.

I. Jesus Picked You Out

The verse describes us as a chosen people whom God picked out. Why? No reason, He just did. Theologians call this *unconditional election*. You did not earn your position in the kingdom of God. There is nothing you can do big enough, brave enough, strong enough, or rich enough to guarantee your place in the family of God. God chose you. Not because of your race or religion or creed or upbringing or skill or education. He chose each of us before the foundation of the world to be holy and blameless in His sight. He predestined us to be adopted into His family:

> Even before he made the world, God loved us and chose us in Christ to be holy and without fault in his eyes. God decided in advance to adopt us into his own family by bringing us to himself through Jesus Christ. This is what he wanted to do, and it gave him great pleasure. (Ephesians 1:4–5)

Jesus told us that we did not choose Him; He chose us. You cannot love others to Jesus Christ until you realize you will never be qualified to earn God's love. It's totally given to us by grace—freely!

2. Jesus Accepted You into His Family

You are a royal priest, God's own possession. Our Father in heaven is the King, and we have a royal bloodline because of it. There is nothing we have done to deserve a position in the kingdom of God; He chose us for His glory:

> And you have caused them to become
> a Kingdom of priests for our God.
> And they will reign on the earth.
> (Revelation 5:10)

3. Jesus Sets You Apart

You are a part of a holy nation. You are not just a run-of-the-mill person. You have been set apart for God. You were created by God and for God. Since God is holy, you are holy. You share His character. The word *holy* means a cut above the crowd, different from society's "norm." You are a holy people. When you do not act with holiness, you are acting out of character. When you live unholy, you contradict the fundamental nature of Christ within you.

4. Jesus Shows You Off

Just as people of wealth enjoy showing off their luxury cars and homes, God proudly displays us, His children, as His very own possessions. At Creation, God intended for everyone to thrive economically, and He wanted us to enjoy the abundance of His generosity. In Genesis chapters

1 and 2, God makes it clear that He planned for humanity to enjoy His creation. However, Adam's and Eve's rebellion had a catastrophic effect on all creation. As a result, people began to live under both a curse and a blessing.

> So God created human beings in his own image. In the image of God, he created them; male and female he created them. (Genesis 1:27)

If we understand that everything we have is God's, we will then be grateful to God. In gratefulness, we give God permission to give us more blessings. Gratitude leads to contentment, and contentment gives God permission to expose His generosity through us.

> But you are not like that, for you are a chosen people. You are royal priests, a holy nation, God's very own possession. As a result, you can show others the goodness of God, for he called you out of the darkness into his wonderful light. (1 Peter 2:9)

5. Jesus Exposes You

He called you out of darkness into His marvelous light, so you are the light of the world. If you are not relating to these facts about yourself as a child of God, it's not because they are beyond your reach. It's because you are living below your privileges. Your assignment often will trigger your inadequacy. It's important for you to remember that Jesus used Peter's failures to turn him from a follower into a leader. Many of the people we read about who became great leaders in the Bible had to be talked into believing they could make a difference.

When God called Moses, Moses said he had a stuttering problem. Jeremiah tried to explain that he was too young to be used by God; and even Gideon said he was the least in his family. God wants to use your feelings of being overwhelmed and inadequate so you will lean on Him. In your weakness, God will shine strong!

When you realize you are a chosen vessel, a royal priest in the kingdom of God, you will want to delete or discard any influences or influencers in your life who distract you from your true purpose. Remember, there is a big difference between *delete* and *discard*. To delete is to remove while discard is to reject.

Maybe you need to delete the access that you have given toxic things and people to your life. Their position in your life has to change as you proceed into your new season. They may still be a part of your life but not sit with you over coffee while you reiterate your mistakes and losses. You are taking new ground and determining who you will choose as a team member.

GETTING UP!

DECLARATION

I once thought that I was not responsible for my healing. Now I know that healing cannot take place unless I allow it. I will no longer allow the hurts to define my life. I am picked by God, accepted by God, and set apart for His glory. I will no longer bleed on people. I will shift the atmosphere with the love of God everywhere that I go.

PRAYER

Jesus,
Thank You for choosing me. Thank You for teaching me how to transition from a hurt mindset to a healed mindset. Turn my weaknesses into opportunities for Your strength to shine through. Help me to see myself the way that You see me. Show me how to walk authentically in who You created me to be.
Amen.

RADICAL RESTORATION

I was introduced to Real Talk Kim in January 2022. I joined the Inner Circle in April 2022. Pastor Kim has changed my life!

I was so broken and following Pastor Kim has caused me to understand why I was broken and how to start repairing myself. I am still a work in progress, but I have been able to set boundaries in my life. I have been able to see why I kept picking the same people with different faces.

My family didn't raise me in church. My mom has never attended church and my dad did for a short period of time. When I was seventeen, I started dating a boy and came home to tell my mom about him. I was so excited. My mom told me that because he was not our color, I needed to break up with him. I was dumbfounded. I had never been taught to judge someone by the color of their skin.

After I broke up with my boyfriend, my mom told my dad. While she was out of town, my dad beat me. I was sent to live with my great-grandmother for months because my father couldn't stand the sight of me. He let me know that I disgusted him.

He took me to a Christian counselor he thought would agree with him about this young man. The counselor did not agree with my father and offered me some very sound advice. He explained that I could walk in forgiveness even when my parents did not understand.

I got baptized in 2015 at thirty-seven years of age. I joined a church and started learning about God. However, my friends couldn't understand how I could follow Jesus and still be friends with them.

When I found Pastor Kim in 2022, I learned why my friends could not continue to walk with me, so I let those friends go. I began serving Jesus on a full-time basis. Thank you, Pastor Kim, for showing me love.

—A

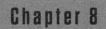

Chapter 8

NEVER TRUST YOUR TONGUE WHEN YOUR HEART IS BITTER

You want God to immediately take away your pain, but that's not how it works. Instead, He's asking you to get up and walk away from it. As I journeyed through my time of healing, I repeatedly cried out to God to please take away the pain. Finally, one night as I lay in my bed crying because of my brokenness, I heard the Lord speak to me in the stillness of my spirit, saying that He was not going to take the pain away.

This was my first time of ever truly sensing the Lord's voice. As a young girl at youth camp, it seemed that every other person had heard the voice of God while I wondered why God did not speak to me. But at this moment, in my darkest hour, I knew I had heard the voice of the Lord.

God gave me the power to release the pain in forgiveness, so it was up to me to let it go. I was learning that there is a process for healing, and you never have to get stuck in the pain. But I had to make the decision to begin the release. I began praying specific prayers of forgiveness for people who had wounded me, consciously and unconsciously. Did it hurt? More than I could have ever imagined.

My parents later described their feelings as they listened to the groanings of a mature thirty-eight-year-old woman, their daughter, whose deliverance went through one phase of self-release after another. They knew God was instructing them to stay out of the process. It was between Him and me.

The deliverance did not happen in a few moments. It had begun weeks, even months, before I determined I could no longer live in the prison of bitterness and unforgiveness that engulfed me. I may have looked like I had it all together; however, I was fighting a war within my emotions that was slowly crippling my entire being.

As I replay those times, I wonder how my boys and my parents felt. I had become so overwhelmed with pain and had allowed it to take over our lives until enough was enough. My parents told me later that they were interceding for me because they knew that the only escape from my inner prison was a total release. I would need to forgive everyone who had inflicted pain, but I also needed to forgive myself for allowing others' choices to dominate and control me.

Sometimes God has to expose what's inside us in order to expand and heal us. For God to give you a new life, He has to disrupt your old one. You probably would like immediate freedom from the bad memories, but that would only happen in a world of make-believe.

You cannot face truth when you are consumed with the what-ifs. We want a balanced world but we live in a world filled with chaos and confusion. It's easy to blame everyone and everything for our mayhem while expecting change to be on the horizon. However, change cannot take place until we determine that we are ready to do what it takes to change.

Each of us is responsible for our decisions, yet we can spend a lifetime blaming everyone else for our mistakes. We've all been hurt, rejected, and betrayed. If you live in the fallen world long enough, you will be lied to and abused, whether physically or emotionally. But what you do with that hurt is more important than the hurt itself. Holding on to the hurt will cause you pain that will keep you from being something new. The choice is completely up to you.

I am a living witness that pain does not release itself; it does not go away on its own. I allowed hurt from broken relationships to control my life far longer than necessary. I had become hard-hearted, bitter, and alone. The moment I chose to begin to change, my entire life took on a whole new meaning. When I realized that if I died, there would be no mourners at my funeral, it was time to act and become who God had created me to be.

You must make a commitment and deliberately begin the process of letting go. I'm not talking about blame shifting, because it's easy to blame others when you are in pain. I'm saying that it's time to take ownership of the pain you have inflicted on others and the pain you've allowed others to pour out on you.

Some things in life break our hearts but fix our vision.

You may have allowed certain people and circumstances to bring chaos and disruption into your life. But times like these bring you to the end of yourself and to the realization that life change is not always bad. I left a house and a business when I knew change was essential. During my season of change, I had two little boys depending on me. I couldn't even figure my own days out, let alone try to figure out how to parent the two little beings God had given me.

Some things in life break our hearts but fix our vision.

In the midst of the confusion of loss and pain, I began seeking Jesus Christ as Lord. It wasn't that I had not been raised to know Jesus. At this point, I had to find God for myself.

As I minister to thousands weekly, I realize that the reason many people stop growing is because they get too comfortable with their lives. Whether you have your life together or it's fragmented, you can become comfortable—even in brokenness. When you stop moving, you become stagnant. Becoming stagnant means there is no longer forward motion in your life. It's possible to become comfortable even when your life is falling apart. A change in location, family situation, job—any kind of change seems impossible.

Before I made the decision to begin my journey of change, at least I had a warm body by my side, even if he was broken as a result of his choices. I may not have known where he was most of the time, but I knew that he would eventually come home. Now, lying in my bed at my parents' house, I was alone and had no idea how to cope. Honestly, I had become comfortable in my pain and rejection.

I had no idea that when I decided to walk away, it would include a season of pruning. I finally began facing the fact that it wasn't only my husband's fault we had hit rock bottom. I had to look in the mirror and see the guilt on my face. I've always heard that it takes two to tango. I get it now. We were both dependent on the broken lifestyle we had created. I could not even see the hardships created for my little boys, who had learned to fend for themselves. If my baby boy had become used to going into the pantry, choosing his meal, and preparing it himself, there was surely a problem. He was only nine years old.

I had become hardened by life's situations and wanted to protect my heart. I could not stay the way I was and be the mom my boys needed. It wasn't my parents' responsibility to raise my sons. So I responded to the still, small voice that I kept hearing from the Holy Spirit.

I knew the pruning was necessary, so it was up to me to allow the Holy Spirit to work in all areas as I surrendered. I realized that sometimes pruning is for discipline and sometimes it's shaping us for the next season. As I watched my mom prune the trees in her yard, I didn't understand why she trimmed branches that were not diseased. Then I realized she was trimming branches that were blocking the light from reaching the other branches. The pruning was for the good of the whole tree.

I knew there was a pruning process taking place in my spirit—things I had allowed to affect my spiritual growth— and that God was getting me ready for a maturing. As He moved within my spirit, even my physical and emotional selves were being transformed. As I look back now, I am more than grateful that God took me through the pruning process. I am now reaching thousands every day and would never have dreamed that my world could be so full of love.

Sometimes there are situations, circumstances, and habits in our lives that are not inherently bad, but they keep us from reaching our full, God-given potential. Pruning isn't always because you're doing something wrong; it can be needed to prepare you for your next season. You definitely don't want to carry anything that weighs you down into a season that is supposed to take you higher. It's important for you to allow God to bring you back into alignment, even when it's uncomfortable.

In the orchard, the farmer clips the ends of healthy branches so they can grow stronger in the next season. If the branches are left unattended, they become too weak to support the fruit. There are times God prunes us so that we can grow inwardly and outwardly become ready for the next level. Pruning helps develop character because charisma will get you in the door, but character is what will keep you there.

We want God to grow what we are doing without changing our lifestyles. When I woke up at my parents' house at my rock bottom, I realized that I had stopped growing. I was not seeking God's will for my life because I had accepted that I could live in the pain. But something inside me knew I couldn't live this way forever, something that said there's more to this life!

THE VALLEY OF BONES

It's amazing that when you are ready for change, God will begin the process. I realize that God is a gentleman. He never forces His will or way into our daily lives. He will, however, walk through the door when invited. Look at the Israelite nation. They were in an impossible situation (Ezekiel 37). They had been conquered by a foreign nation. Their cities were burned, the temple destroyed, and the entire nation had been expelled into captivity. Yet, God had a plan. He reminded the children of Israel through the prophet Ezekiel that He was the God of the impossible.

> The LORD took hold of me, and I was carried away by the Spirit of the LORD to a valley filled with bones. He led me all around among the bones that covered the valley floor. They were scattered everywhere across the ground and were completely dried out. Then he asked me, "Son of man, can these bones become living people again?"
>
> "O Sovereign LORD," I replied, "you alone know the answer to that."
>
> Then he said to me, "Speak a prophetic message to these bones and say, 'Dry bones, listen to the word of the LORD! This is what the Sovereign LORD says: Look! I am going to put breath into you and make you live again! I will put flesh and muscles on you and cover you with skin. I will put breath into you, and you will come to life. Then you will know that I am the LORD.'"
>
> So I spoke this message, just as he told me. Suddenly as I spoke, there was a rattling noise all across the valley.

The bones of each body came together and attached themselves as complete skeletons. Then as I watched, muscles and flesh formed over the bones. Then skin formed to cover their bodies, but they still had no breath in them.

Then he said to me, "Speak a prophetic message to the winds, son of man. Speak a prophetic message and say, 'This is what the Sovereign LORD says: Come, O breath, from the four winds! Breathe into these dead bodies so they may live again.'"

So, I spoke the message as he commanded me, and breath came into their bodies. They all came to life and stood up on their feet—a great army. (Ezekiel 37:1–10)

Ezekiel was taken to the valley of dry bones, which represented the Israelite nation. The people had been conquered, their cities destroyed, and they were in exile. They had no hope. But God was showing Ezekiel that even though Israel had lost everything, there was still hope. God showed this prophet the dry bones. He told him that this is as bad as you can get. There was no life left, no skin, no resuscitation possible, no way these bones could be restored in the natural.

It sounds like so many situations where we give up and live life on autopilot. Then God sends someone or something into our lives to resuscitate us. It is one thing to believe God for a miracle to heal the sick or maybe even raise the dead. It's something else when you walk into a valley of dry bones and God begins saying that He is ready to bring things back to life. Situations can go past the point of no return—job loss, death, sickness, marriage failure. But God can turn every hopeless situation around in an instant.

God told Ezekiel to prophesy over the dry bones and command them to accept life and come back together. The bones began taking shape again—skin, tendons, and muscles reappeared. But even with the reshaping of these bones, they still had no life. Then God told Ezekiel to command breath into these dry bones that had come back together. Do you believe these bones sprang back to life, stood up on their feet, and became as a mighty army? God was letting Ezekiel know that the Israelites would be restored when they had lost everything and saw no way out.

I wonder how many times you have been in such a predicament, had no way out, yet God supernaturally turned your life around. I know that, even today, as I watch my twenty-eight-year-old son lead worship and the congregation moves with him, I am overwhelmed with gratitude that God would cover my boys when their parents were not doing their job to protect them.

My ex-husband and I were so broken that we could not see the pain and devastation our boys were experiencing. However, when I moved them out of their home, school, city, and away from their friends, I began to see anger, resentment, and hopelessness manifest. My boys were acting out of the pain they had been experiencing within our family. We had been too busy fighting, trying to maintain a semblance of normalcy, and just paying the bills.

I am so thankful that I made the decision to change—my life, my home, my city, my marriage. When I began realizing that I did not have to stay stuck any longer, I knew God was assisting me in my change. I was ready for a makeover from the inside out, and God had been waiting on me.

I would never have believed that, fifteen years later, I could walk in such forgiveness. The bitterness that had overwhelmed my being and caused me to be full of anger and unforgiveness is now under the blood of Jesus. I pray for my enemies and love others in a way that I never imagined possible. My family—even my boys, who walked very carefully in my presence because they never knew what type of language would come out of my mouth—now love spending time with me.

GETTING UP!

DECLARATION

I once thought I was unable to obtain my freedom. Now I know that I am getting up and walking away from my pain. I have been made whole through the blood of Jesus Christ. I release every piece of pain I have been holding on to and welcome the healing power of God within me. I will keep my heart free from bitterness and my words sweet and life-giving.

PRAYER

Jesus,
Thank You for being the perfect example of how to walk in love instead of bitterness. I want to be quick to forgive and not get hung up on the wrongs done to me. Show me how to forgive seventy times seven just as You instructed Your disciples. Help me to stay free from all things that would jade my heart so that I can walk right before You.
Amen.

RADICAL RESTORATION

I am excited to share with you how much Pastor Kim has influenced my life for the better and helped me to find my voice again. I can relate to her in so many ways, being raised a pastor's kid myself. Trying to find my own voice and path, I didn't want others to think that my faith was handed to me or that I am just following in my dad's footsteps. I want people to know me for who I am and for who God has called me to be in this life.

I had seen Pastor Kim going live each morning and wanted to click on so many times but, I had taken her for her name on Facebook (REAL TALK KIM) and was intimidated. Once I started to get to know Pastor Kim, I began to see her heart and how big it shines in all that she does. I knew that God had connected me to her platform for a reason because I needed that real talk about how it was and how it was going to continue to be until I got the courage to stand up and allow God to heal those past traumas, hurts, and insecurities that I carried around for years. I began to get to know

Pastor Kim through her sermons, podcasts, and prayer calls. I felt God open the door for me to join the RTK Inner Circle, and I won't lie, I tried to outrun it.

When I first met Pastor Kim, I let her know I was in her Inner Circle. She hugged me and made me feel seen, heard, and loved. God confirmed for me that this was my pastor and, ever since then, I have been serving at Limitless.

Pastor Kim is leading a movement and raising up fearless leaders in the kingdom of God. She is truly an inspiration and loved by so many! Pastor Kim, thank you. You are helping me to pivot so much in my life and to really trust the process of becoming all that God has called me to be. You have my support, prayers, and love.

—V

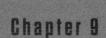

Chapter 9

CHANGE YOUR HEART, CHANGE YOUR LIFE

When Myspace was the favorite online social media app, I was trying to get to know myself by answering a survey called "Twenty-Five Random Things About Me." People would list their favorite things and other facts about themselves. The problem was I could not answer any of the questions, not even, What is your favorite color? I realized I had no favorites because I was like a chameleon, changing colors with my environment. I had no idea who I was, so how in the world could I become something better?

Five days later, my youngest son, Lyncoln, presented me with the most precious gift I have ever received. He had written me a poem, dressed it up on beautiful paper in a gorgeous frame, and gift-wrapped it because it was Mother's Day.

It read:

> You are beautiful, you are kind
> You love me when I am annoying
> You sing like an angel
> You buy me things
> You work hard for my needs, you provide
>   for me . . .

I began to weep when I read, "You survived hell in high heels . . ." He ended with "My favorite thing that I love about you is that . . . You are you." Lyncoln gave me this poem at the lowest point in my life. I had no direction and no instructions on how to break free, and yet, I made up my mind that day to do whatever was necessary to become the best me I could be for my boys. Because of his poem, my ministry was initially called Conquering Hell in High Heels.

He often chooses those with the worst pasts to create the best futures.

No matter how much it hurts now, one day you will look back and realize that changing your heart changed your life for the better. When you understand there is purpose in your pain, you will begin moving forward. Faith without action is not faith at all; it's just wishful thinking. Put feet to your faith!

It's amazing how you cannot change your heart without changing your actions. Whatever we think about the most is what our lives will become. Think about this as you begin processing your next thought pattern. Do you normally lean to the negative or the positive? Is your glass half full or half empty? On a given day, do you find yourself on a peak, in a pit, or somewhere in between? Our mindsets can keep us stuck, or we can shift them in order to shift our direction.

We would love to remain on the peaks of life—those times of extreme joy and gladness. Wouldn't that be nice? But that's just not reality. Unfortunately, many people spend their time in the pit of emotional despair, financial hardship, mental anguish, physical pain, or something else just as draining. It's even more unfortunate that many people park in that pit and never get out. Discouraged and defeated, they decide to remain where they are instead of determining to escape the hole and climb up to the next peak.

The apostle Paul is a great example of someone who could face physical and emotional anguish and still keep his focus on winning Gentiles to Christ. Even though Paul became a follower of Jesus Christ and wrote over half the New Testament, he found himself in his own pit—in the form of a ship tossed in a raging storm. Paul was being taken to Rome to be tried as a political rebel, but the ship carrying 274 people was caught up in a violent storm and wrecked on the island of Malta. All passengers on board were able to swim safely to shore.

This is where the story gets interesting.

Once ashore, they discovered that the island of Malta was inhabited by a group of people who welcomed the wayfaring strangers with a warm fire. As Paul gathered sticks to assist the natives in building the fire, a poisonous viper viciously bit him. The natives were watching. They knew

Paul would surely die from the poisonous bite. Paul, however, shook the viper loose and went on about his business. I wonder how many situations could have been celebrated instead of tolerated if we had only shaken off the "poisonous vipers" in our lives.

The story didn't end with the viper; in fact, the viper catapulted Paul into his next season. The same natives who thought Paul was a murderer and was only getting what he deserved now realized he was unlike any of the other men who had come ashore. They questioned who this man could be who had shaken a viper off his arm and just kept living as though nothing happened? *He must be a god*, they thought.

This presented Paul with the opportunity to meet Publius, the leading citizen of Malta. Paul and his friends stayed in the home of Publius for three days, and during this time, Paul prayed for Publius's father and he was healed. Publius was converted to Christianity and a revival broke out on the island.

> As it happened, Publius's father was ill with fever and dysentery. Paul went in and prayed for him, and laying his hands on him, he healed him. Then all the other sick people on the island came and were healed. As a result we were showered with honors, and when the time came to sail, people supplied us with everything we would need for the trip. (Acts 28:8–10)

Paul was able to turn a pit into a peak because he refused to stay stuck when he could walk victoriously and free. Yes, he was still a prisoner, but he refused to allow his physical limitations to imprison his emotions. Having freedom doesn't mean we will never have trials; it simply means that when we do, we can choose how we will react. I wonder how many times we allow our circumstances to determine our altitude because of our attitude.

I have heard people say many times that God will not give you more than you can handle. First Corinthians 10:13 tells us that God will not allow *temptation* to be more than we can stand; He will show us a way out:

> The temptations in your life are no different from what others experience. And God is faithful. He will not allow the temptation to be more than you can stand. When you are tempted, he will show you a way out so that you can endure.

When you are feeling the pressures of life, feeling ill-equipped and weak, don't be so hard on yourself. God knows you are human, He knows life is hard and sometimes it just hurts. Some things in life will break your heart and take your breath away. Some things will knock you on your butt and make you feel like you don't have the strength to get back up. Some situations can be so devastating that you can't even think about tomorrow, so how on earth can you plan for next week? You are doing well to survive moment by moment.

It's easy to feel tempted to quit, throw in the towel, and lose faith. That won't get you anywhere! But you can also choose to see the glass half full and know that God has already provided the way out. The reason I spend hours daily on social media, Zoom calls, and one-on-one sessions with hurting people is because I was stuck in a life of brokenness, aloneness, pain, rejection, and betrayal. Then I came to the end of me and knew it was no longer a choice to stay stuck.

I am convinced that I would not even be able to make it from day to day without the Lord Jesus who picked me up, turned my life upside down, and then right side up. How do I know that the Lord Jesus will download His peace that passes understanding, His supernatural strength, and His power and grace to sustain you through trials? Because He did it for me! I was no poster child for being an obedient daughter to parents who raised me to love and serve Jesus. It seemed that every situation I chose to step into was one more act of failure rather than a progression into maturity.

The Bible was my source of strength in my time of brokenness, the same book I had chosen to ignore while attending Christian schools and church weekly. My mother ended each day with my brother and me sitting together reading chapters from the Good Book and then praying over us for peaceful sleep. When I finally hit my lowest point and knew there was no other way, I was determined to study and understand the stories in the Bible.

I found that when I am weak, He is strong. I found that when I felt God had given me more than I could handle, I could allow Him to handle it. I borrowed His strength, His wisdom, His comfort. I finally understood that He has more than enough for me because He is the God of more than enough. God doesn't ask you to carry the weight of your circumstances alone. He calls to you, saying:

"Come to me, all of you who are weary and carry heavy burdens, and I will give you rest." (Matthew 11:28)

When you are stuck, what is one of the top issues you face? You've probably heard "a person's closest friends are a projection of their future." It's easy to stay stuck when your friends are stuck with you. People who do not have anything going for themselves will only bring you down to their level. It's important for you to surround yourself with people who will help elevate you to the next level, people who are driven to succeed in life.

It's amazing how you can surround yourself with addicts, quitters, and haters and not realize how quickly your life can spiral out of control. When you determine what you want your future to look like, you can then make decisions to remove those people from your life who are not assisting in your growth.

On my one-hour commutes back and forth to my job each morning and evening, I determined I had one choice to make: to be free. Instead of listening to those who ministered to my flesh, I began listening to preaching and teaching with Bishop T. D. Jakes, Joyce Meyer, and others who ministered to my spirit and directed me in the way I had determined I would go:

Don't be fooled by those who say such things, for "bad company corrupts good character." (1 Corinthians 15:33)

Jesus can redeem time that you have lost. He often chooses those with the worst pasts to create the best futures. Understand that what happens to your friends doesn't have to dictate and determine what happens to you. We have all been let down by people we depended on who ended up not being there when we needed them the most.

The end of me is where I found the God who changed my world.

It's only natural to go through life overcompensating because those closest to you have labeled you or put you in a box that you now call your home. The enemy believes that if he can keep you believing those labels, you will never break out of the box, change your heart, and change your life. Why? Because God chose you from the foundation of the world. He knew you would eventually redeem your lost years:

> You saw me before I was born.
> Every day of my life was recorded in
>   your book.
> Every moment was laid out
>   before a single day had passed.
>
> (PSALM 139:16)

When you feel inadequate and think you could never succeed, it's important to remember that God already knows your future. For a heart change, you must slow down and quit bleeding on people who didn't cut you. Why blame others for mistakes you have made? It won't fix anything; it will just prolong the healing process. The answer to your next season is to take ownership of your failures, your betrayals, and your rejections, and simply forgive yourself for allowing those seasons to define you.

Are you in the wrong crowd? At the wrong place? Wrong time? Are you allowing labels to stop you from succeeding? You are chosen! You are God's own possession and masterpiece.

How do you view yourself? You need an understanding of who you are in God:

> But you are not like that, for you are a chosen people. You are royal priests, a holy nation, God's very own possession. As a result, you can show others the goodness of God, for he called you out of the darkness into his wonderful light. (1 Peter 2:9)

Peter said that when we realize our full potential, we can show others the goodness of God. It cannot happen until we come to the end of ourselves. The end of me is where I found the God who changed my world. Would I do it all over again? Absolutely! I have learned to love the woman I allowed God to change, shape, and mold. I have honor and respect for the woman I am today. When I look in the mirror, I see a godly, righteous, whole woman who determines to live life fully and take as many people to heaven with her as possible. I refuse to allow people in my life who would try to steal my joy or delay my purpose.

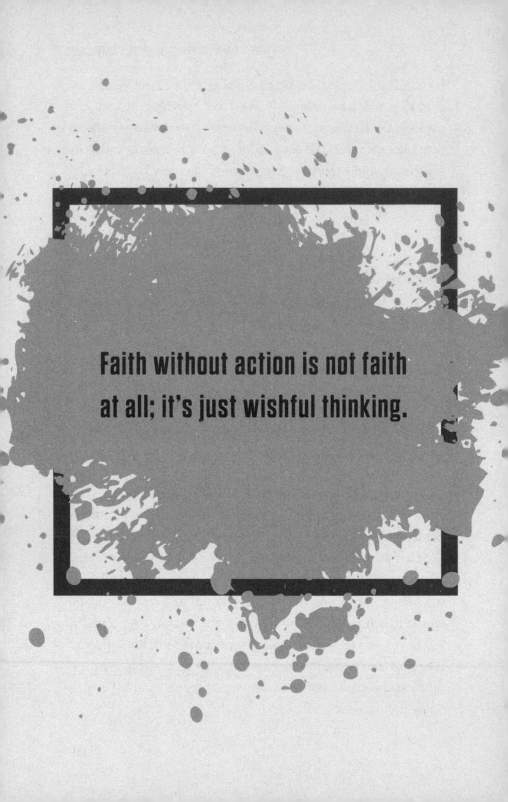

Faith without action is not faith at all; it's just wishful thinking.

HOW DOES GOD VIEW YOU?

Let's reinforce what God says about you.

You Are Enough. You Are Chosen.

You need an understanding of who you are in Christ. You are enough because Jesus called you before you were even born—you are chosen. When you begin defending your position or allowing others to determine your way, you are sabotaging your destiny. You are chosen, not because of race, sex, culture, or education. God chose you before He created the world. It's important for you to understand that you did not choose Him, He chose you.

> Even before he made the world, God loved us and chose us in Christ to be holy and without fault in his eyes. God decided in advance to adopt us into his own family by bringing us to himself through Jesus Christ. This is what he wanted to do, and it gave him great pleasure. (Ephesians 1:4–5)

You Have a Savior

God loved you so much that He sent His only Son to die in your place. You were adopted into God's family through Jesus Christ. He suffered the humiliation and pain of dying on a cross so that you could have everlasting life. You cannot save yourself. Jesus suffered for doing good without retaliating toward those who mistreated Him to achieve His mission of your salvation:

> He personally carried our sins
>> in his body on the cross
> so that we can be dead to sin
>> and live for what is right.
> By his wounds
>> you are healed.
>
> (1 PETER 2:24)

We would have remained lost in our sins if Jesus had not willingly endured this injustice. This perfect man suffered an excruciating death so we could have eternal life. On the cross, Jesus carried our sins. He died in our place. Not only did He give His life as a sacrifice for our lives, but He also suffered the wounds in His body for our healing so that we could walk in wholeness.

You Have a Mediator: Jesus

Jesus Christ is the One who cleanses every believer's guilt, stands on their behalf, and guarantees eternal life. This God-who-became-man offered Himself up as a living sacrifice for our sins. It's not about each of us making the change; it's about allowing Jesus Christ to be Lord of our lives, then accepting that He will never leave us nor forsake us. He promises to be with us until the end. The end of what? Time, sickness, and death.

> There is one God and one Mediator who can reconcile God and humanity—the man Christ Jesus. (1 Timothy 2:5)

You Are Set Apart

When you understand that God specifically chose you for a purpose that no one can fill but you, you will understand that you have been *set apart*. You are unlike any other member of your family. You may share the same DNA, but Jesus Christ has specifically picked you out for this exact time. You will never be perfect; however, you can be righteous because of Jesus' sacrifice for you. You can confess and release sin while allowing Jesus Christ to be your Lord and Savior.

> "And I will forgive their wickedness, and I will never again remember their sins." (Hebrews 8:12)

Unconfessed sin is a burden that weighs you down. When you confess your sin to God, He lifts it off your shoulders, rolls it away, and it disappears.

You Are Called Out of Darkness by Jesus

Jesus will call you out of the bar where you have been *nae-naeing* instead of pray-praying. Your assignment will trigger inadequacy, yet you carry the oil of anointing that will set you up for your next season. You may have been sitting in a boardroom as CEO of a company when you sensed change coming. You may be a full-time mom who has seen her world fall apart and is experiencing unavoidable change.

When the enemy sees change in you, he begins his strategy. He will try to wear you out with issues that you haven't dealt with, so be honest with yourself on this journey. Sometimes it's easier to forgive others than to forgive yourself for things you have allowed. The enemy cannot steal your calling, so he will make you doubt that God has given you one! But Jesus has called you out of darkness and called you into light.

Trust yourself. Know that you have a purpose and God has seen it from the beginning of time. You may have lived a life of "less than," trusting no one and not understanding that it just takes one *yes*!

When Moses was called by God, he was full of excuses for why he could not lead the Israelites out of the nation of Egypt. Moses said, "I stutter when I speak" (Exodus 4:10). God said, "I will give you Aaron to stand by your side" (v. 14). Jeremiah said, "I'm too young" (Jeremiah 1:6). Despite his age, God said that He would be with him (v. 8).

When God has called you, He promises to be with you. He makes your mess a message and places the right people in your life to walk with you.

GETTING UP!

DECLARATION

I once thought change was impossible, but now I know that I am saying yes to change! I know that sometimes God shakes things up to place me on a better path because He sees from the beginning to the end. God has made me enough and chose me before I was born. I let go of the box that I put my life in, and I am ready to walk in a new direction.

PRAYER

Jesus,
Thank You for always taking care of my heart. I want to reach my full potential in You. Show me the areas in my life that need to change. Expose anything in my life that would hinder me in this process. Give me the courage to do the hard things.
Amen.

PART III
PRISON BREAK

Referred to as a *bust out*, a *breakout*, an *escape*, it is normally an illegal way

to break free of your confined place. When we are dealing with situations

that are holding us hostage, it can become a legal escape when we find the

means to change situations and even people who have caused us to be stuck.

RADICAL RESTORATION

A friend from church introduced me to RTK in June 2022, and as soon as I opened the link, I was catapulted to a new height in Christ! The similarities between us were glaringly obvious from the very start, so I signed up for the Inner Circle. We're both alpha females, bold, and love fashion. We both also worked at Bloomingdale's, are barrier breakers, have struggled with addiction, and have an intense anointing from El Shaddai.

Here was a power female expressing her whole self and not apologizing for being who God made her to be.

RTK's messages instantly brought new rivers of life to my being that have been renewing, uplifting, and life changing, positively making me so much stronger in Christ and for others. I'm also recommitted to sobriety, which had been a long time coming. Everything RTK says, happens in my life! She has a right-now word all the time! She's an apostolic prophetess who's raising up an army of world-changing champions, and I'm now in that number. What a blessing she is to the body of Christ, empowering others to be their authentic selves for God.

—T

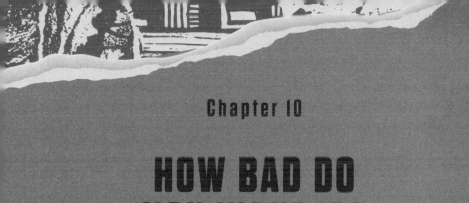

Chapter 10

HOW BAD DO YOU WANT IT?

Have you ever had an "oh, hell no" moment? In the Gospel of Mark, there was a woman who had an "oh, hell no" moment after she had been bleeding for twelve years. She was desperate to be made well, so she decided she would do whatever was necessary to touch the hem of Jesus' garment. She went against the press of the crowd. She joined the throngs crowding Jesus even though she was unclean. Sometimes you've got to let people misunderstand you. She was supposed to be quarantined or sheltering in isolation. Yet, she was sick and tired of being sick and tired.

Your issue may be that you're entangled in a business or personal relationship that has stolen your dreams, surrounded you in darkness, and you see no way to escape. The relationship you thought would motivate you to be the best you is stifling your life's breath without the hope of relief.

You may have poured your life into a company that is going nowhere and failing fast. Yet still, it has been easier to remain locked in place because you have no vision for your next move.

You may have spent your entire life giving your all to those called family, and now that they have reached their success, they've decided to ditch you. They no longer need your financial and emotional input and are moving on without you!

It's easy to get stuck in your present as others move on without you. You may not feel needed as the go-to person any longer; however, you can still make a choice to keep moving as God brings other relationships into your life.

I can tell you that for change to come, you have to do your part. *You gotta get up!* Understanding the story of the woman with the issue of blood will help you get motivated to move. Your greatest blessing in getting up will first be the place of your greatest frustration.

> For she thought to herself, "If I can just touch his robe, I will be healed." (Mark 5:28)

This unnamed woman thought to herself, *If I can just touch Him.* Do you realize how much time you spend every day in thinking negatively about the what-ifs in your life? For her to begin moving, she had to release her negative thinking and determine it was time for change.

It's not easy to get untangled from the destructive thought webs that have caused you to feel lost with no hope, especially when all you have heard is that you are an outcast. This woman was not allowed around the general public because she was marked as unclean. It didn't matter that she did nothing to deserve her sickness; she still carried the stigma of the disease. Everyone knew she was sick. Everyone knew the source of her sickness. She had been bleeding for 4,380 days. She heard Jesus was in town and something shifted in her. She made the choice to get free.

During those 4,380 days, she had gone to every doctor who had been recommended for her condition and no one could give her any relief. She probably had been pacified by the best of the best in the medical field of that day and had tried numerous remedies. But nothing worked. However, she had heard about the man with the deformed hand, who had been healed on the Sabbath by a man called Jesus.

All Jesus did was instruct the man to stretch out his hand. Jesus had noticed his condition and called him out. It was the right time and the right place. Jesus said to this man, "Stretch out your hand," and it was restored. Just one moment of obedience changed his life forever (Mark 3).

And there was the man who had been living among the tombs and was possessed by an evil spirit. He lived in the burial caves and could not be restrained by anyone. But then Jesus came by. The man was alone because he could not live among his family and friends. He was out of control. He wandered day and night among the caves, howling and cutting himself with sharp stones.

When Jesus arrived at the caves, the evil spirit in this man cried out and begged Jesus not to torture him. The evil spirit knew the power of Jesus Christ. The evil spirit begged for mercy after Jesus told him to come out of the man. Jesus asked the evil spirit's name and was told that it was Legion because there were so many evil spirits inside this man whom everyone had thought was insane. All it took for this man to gain his freedom was one word from Jesus (Mark 5).

The woman with the issue of blood heard about the daughter of Jairus, the leader of the local synagogue. This little girl was dying when her father approached Jesus, pleading for Him to heal her. Everyone knew Jesus was on His way to Jairus's house when the crowd surrounded Him. In that crowd was the woman with the issue of blood. She knew people did not want her to be in the public square among them, but she knew the only way to find healing would be to touch Jesus.

Everyone's demands had imprisoned her long enough. The shift came when she thought, *I've got to do what I've never done.* She had never allowed herself to be out and among the crowd because they had expected her to stay locked up and covered. But this woman determined she had to move. Immediately after touching the hem of Jesus' garment, the bleeding stopped, and she knew she was healed. She felt the healing anointing in her body (Mark 5).

Can you imagine her excitement turning into trepidation as she was moving away from Jesus and He began asking, "Who touched me?" His disciples were trying to appease Him by telling Him there were too many people around Him. Everyone was touching Him. They had no idea what He was really asking. Yet Jesus kept asking. She was frightened of the crowd and trembling as she came to the realization that Jesus was going to keep asking until she came forward. So she made her way through the crowd and confessed that she was the guilty party. She had no idea what would happen next:

And he said to her, "Daughter, your faith has made you well. Go in peace. Your suffering is over." (Mark 5:34)

Jesus let her know that her suffering was over because she had moved in faith. You might think that you are waiting on God when He is actually waiting on you. There are many examples of faith in action in the Bible. I understand through my own experiences that God will allow you to be in the middle of your own hell and still breathe because He is giving you the chance to do your part, to flip your script. He expects you to help yourself while allowing Him to be the Lord of your life, your decisions, and your actions.

You cannot do it alone. You must have accountability, people in your life who tell you the truth—your pastor, mentor, or a friend. Most of my problems were created because I refused to allow God and those who offered godly counsel to help guide my actions. The words *honor* and *respect* were foreign to my vocabulary. *Rebellion* is the best word to describe most of my actions that caused me to end up single with two boys at the age of thirty-six.

I personally called it *independent*, being my own boss. I refused to be dependent on anyone. I repeatedly told my sons' father, whom I truly loved for years, that I didn't need a man . . . until one day, I didn't have one. All because I lived with the fear of being abandoned or heartbroken.

I knew I was attempting to protect myself from the very thing that eventually caught up to me. I was left alone with two boys, moving into my parents' home seven hours from my boys' school, home, and friends.

Just normal. That's all my boys wanted. A normal family where their parents were not screaming at each other whenever they were together. A normal family who would sit down together in the evening for a meal or just go out for a movie. They have no fond memories of our lives back then, but, thank God, He has given me time to begin making good memories. I've heard that you will never forget the bad memories, but I remember my dad saying that you can create enough new memories that they will overshadow anything that has caused you sadness.

In this season of my life, I realize there is a vast difference between being codependent and interdependent. *Codependence* is an unequal partnership that puts one person above another while *interdependence* is a relationship in which a partner can retain their identity and still value the other person.

I had failed at keeping a marriage together and was unable to continue providing for my family on the same level as before. I could not give my boys a cozy homelife, so I gave them toys and anything else that would help reassure them that they were living in a normal home. But what was normal?

I was the provider, and my husband was being "kept." I let everyone know that it was "normal" for him to be a house husband and stay home all day while I brought in the funds. It is amazing that God did still sufficiently take care of us. I'm sure it was because of our praying parents.

There were those times when my husband would just

disappear and be gone for several months. I remember living in daily fear of what might happen if he didn't come back.

I finally realized our relationship must end. I then made a decision that would dramatically change the scope of my life. I picked up my phone, called my parents, and finally asked for help.

Their independent prodigal daughter, who had only allowed them to be involved in the ways she chose, was finally confessing that her life was out of control. My husband left that night as he had many times before, but I knew our lives would never be the same.

My dad put my mom on the first plane out the next morning and, upon arriving, she immediately began getting my family ready to move. I was on the brink of a total nervous breakdown, and everyone who came into my home acknowledged that my world was upside down.

How can you live in a $500,000 home, drive a Mercedes convertible, and look like you have conquered the world while simultaneously losing everything that you have worked so hard to obtain? My mind was so distorted with loss that it seemed as if I were losing everything.

If you had told me that weekend that I was stepping into the greatest season of my life, I would have given you choice words to counteract anything positive you could say. In my darkness I could not see that there was going to be a light at the end of my tunnel. Now, fourteen years later, I am preaching in megachurches throughout the United States and even pastoring the church that my parents passed on to me.

In your pain, you must activate faith with action to see change. Make a conscious decision. A momentary change.

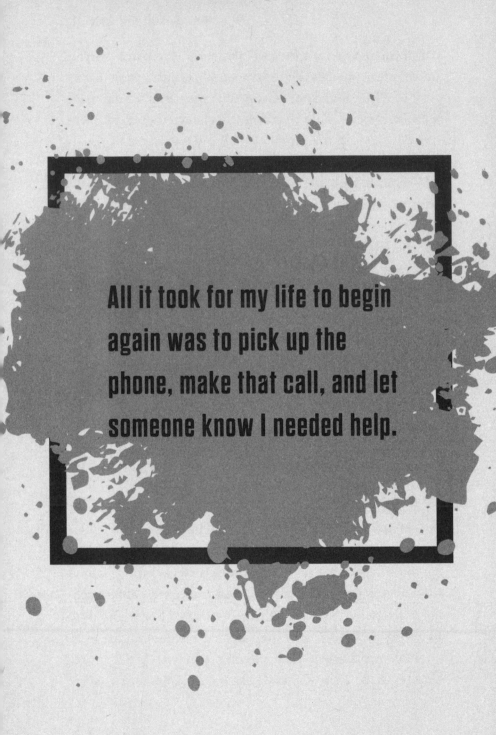

All it took for my life to begin again was to pick up the phone, make that call, and let someone know I needed help.

All it took for my life to begin again was to pick up the phone, make that call, and let someone know I needed help.

WHAT'S YOUR DIAGNOSIS?

The woman with the issue of blood had to go through the season of diagnosis. All we are told is that she had an issue of blood. We don't know specifics, only that she bled for twelve years. What is your diagnosis? Is it divorce, relationship problems, sickness, constant pain, loss of income? If you can't diagnosis it, don't be angry when no one can help you.

Be careful not to burn too many bridges because you'll have no one to help you during difficult seasons. I'm talking about healthy accountability. It's easy to listen to unqualified people who were never meant to diagnose you. But what happens when everyone in your life looks and thinks just like you?

When I left my old life, I left my old friends who had hung out with me on girls night at the bar. Anyone who partied with me or was part of that dark season could not go with me into my new season. I remember lying in my bed alone and crying out to God that everyone knew how far I had fallen and how much I had lost.

I was embarrassed because I was the only member of my family who had gone through a divorce. I knew the naysayers were discussing my doom and I wasn't even able to take the stand and plead my case. As I cried out for mercy to Jesus, He instructed me to live as though I had never sinned because He had taken my sins to the cross and I had been made righteous.

> He personally carried our sins
> in his body on the cross
> so that we can be dead to sin
> and live for what is right.
> By his wounds
> you are healed.
>
> (1 PETER 2:24)

This woman with the issue of blood could not see through her pain of loss, rejection, and embarrassment to recognize that she was a walking miracle. She had bled for twelve long years yet she was still alive.

She had suffered a great deal from many doctors, and over the years she had spent everything she had to pay them, but she had gotten no better. She had gotten worse (Mark 5:25).

The doctors had no idea what was causing the blood flow nor how to stop it, yet they continually scheduled appointment after appointment with no relief until she had spent everything she had. There was no apparent reason for her sickness and, as far as we know, it was not as a result of any type of sin. She had done nothing to deserve this, yet she lived with it every day.

Her problem was bleeding. What is your problem? Could it be your constant complaining or arguing or just living negatively? It could be living in comparison to those in your life who do not even know your middle name. Maybe you're not fully bleeding; maybe you're just leaking here and there. Did your family and friends give up on you because *you* gave up on you? Maybe you're incapable of moving on. You have lived broken for so long that *normal* is not a word in your vocabulary. I get it. I lived that way so long that broken was my normal.

I remember times my husband came in and immediately begin throwing whatever he could pick up against the wall or down the stairs. However, by noon the next day, there was no evidence that we had gone through an explosive night of arguing. I would bring the laborers in and have them make my house like new again. If there was no evidence, then our lives must be normal. We could cope through another day.

What are you doing about the leak in your life? You have to do your part to see change. Satan uses different mirrors to keep you hostage in your world of broken. For most of us, we must live in the tension between what we see with our eyes (appearance) and the promises of God (truth).

As Christians we have access to the truth and have authority through the Holy Spirit. We have the victory. The devil knows he is fighting a losing battle every time he comes against the children of God.

SATAN'S MIRRORS

Mirror of Forgetfulness

We can live through a season of hell on earth and, when the atmosphere shifts momentarily, it's easy to forget the pain, the rejection, and the betrayal that had taken over our existence. Maybe life is changing. Maybe that significant other has been set free from his or her anger. Maybe the bank won't foreclose the loan. Maybe I won't lose my job. Living in a world of maybes.

Mirror of Depression

It's easier to go to bed and stay there with the covers wrapped around my body than to deal with issues that I have no idea how to change. Life is too hard. I'll never be able to move on from this issue.

Mirror of Insanity

Keep that doctor's appointment to get whatever can be prescribed to isolate the depression, the oppression, the loneliness. It's easier to cover up the pain than to deal with the pain. I just need something to help me sleep so I don't have to deal.

Mirror of Death

Hopelessness becomes the normal reaction to any life situation. There's no way out.

The woman with the issue of blood was a victim of gross sickness for twelve years. What is the duration of your pain? How long have you tried everything, and everything has failed? I remember my parents singing a song that went, "If you've tried everything and everything has failed, try Jesus." That sounds too elementary, too simple to be true, yet it worked for me. I had tried everything in my power to change situations, people, and other things, and nothing had worked. I finally came to the end of myself and realized I needed God.

The woman had been carrying this sickness so long that I'm sure it became who she was. She had to prepare herself for the stigma, the embarrassment, the fear of the blood coming through her garments and everyone seeing what she was contending with as she made her way to Jesus. She knew they knew, yet she still must have wanted to hide her embarrassment. Those close to you probably know that you have been dealing with your situation much longer than you have thought.

This woman had spent all her earnings on doctors and medication, and nothing had worked. She was isolated from the love of friends, family, and neighbors. When you are hiding pain, you easily begin to isolate yourself because you don't want others to know the real damage you've experienced.

After twelve years, this woman knew the medical professionals had no cure. There were no other specialists she could try. Her only hope was this man called Jesus. My only hope when I finally came to the realization that my life could not continue as it had been was a whisper to the Lord Jesus for help and then a phone call to my parents. I remembered the call I had received from my mom one year prior to my moment of decision. She had let me know that, in prayer, the Lord had told her to call and ask me one question: "Is the life you are living now what you want in twenty years?"

She shook my world that day, and I continually thought

about that question. I stayed on my roller coaster of ups and downs for another year before I finally determined it was time to get off.

I realized that in my pain I was bleeding on people who had not cut me. I realized that the life I had thought was normal was so far from that. People I dealt with daily had no idea the pain that I carried inside. To numb the pain, I would drink myself into oblivion because I had no idea how to change my normal. But all it took was one decision.

That one decision led to change. Change, which was the most uncomfortable season of my life, was the greatest opportunity for me to become acquainted with the woman I am today. I wanted to get well. I was desperate for change. I would do whatever was necessary to see this change take place.

You don't have to do it alone. God has placed people in your life who will walk along beside you and be there for comfort and support. Just do your part. All it takes is that one decision.

GETTING UP!

DECLARATION

I once thought I had to stay stuck in dysfunction. Now I know my "oh, hell no" moment has come! I will no longer put up with the things the enemy has used as distraction. I will no longer repeat the same cycles. God, with Your help, I am getting up and moving! I no longer have to settle for the "diagnosis" because I know that You are the cure.

PRAYER

Jesus,
Thank You for being the ultimate healer. I am willing to do what it takes to walk in wholeness. Thank You for having Your hand upon my life even while going through hard seasons. Help me turn these tests into testimonies. Use my life as a witness to others to show them that they can also overcome with You by their side.
Amen.

RADICAL RESTORATION

I am a part of the RTK Inner Circle, and I am so in love with Pastor Kim! She is real, raw, and relevant! In 2012, all the trauma from being abused physically, sexually, mentally, and emotionally started to manifest itself. I am not sure who I was running faster from, God or myself. In 2018, broke, busted, and disgusted, I packed all my belongings in the trunk of my car and headed to New Jersey. It was there I had my dark night of the soul and dug at every root I had in order to heal. In 2020 I moved back to Wisconsin, my ex-husband and I reconnected, and my family has since been fully restored!

I identify with PK on every level, and she helps me to be my best self every day. Recently I was set free from bulimia, which I have battled for two decades. Pastor Kim teaches us that the way you start a season determines how you finish it. I did not want to start 2023 as I had always started my new years. I *decided* to finish the year stronger than ever so I can continue in strength every year hereafter. I enrolled in a Spanish class, I work out six days a week, gave up the booze, and changed my diet entirely! I have lost fifteen pounds and I am back running again and I haven't done that in years! I am one of the many lives that have been changed by Pastor Kim. My life's dream is to be a motivational speaker. PK is one of the people I want to meet most in this world, and one day I hope to speak on the same platform with her.

—N

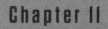

Chapter 11

EITHER I GROW WITH YOU OR I OUTGROW YOU

Waiting on others to walk in agreement with you will keep you stagnant and disappointed. Stop allowing people to determine your direction when the Bible says you can do all things through Christ who strengthens you (Philippians 4:13). Stop waiting for people to validate you when God validated you before you were born.

> Stop waiting for people to validate you when God validated you before you were born.

Think about the young men Jesus chose to walk with Him—His disciples. This group was formed to carry out His mission on earth. They would travel with Him for three years and be entrusted to carry His mission forward after the day of Pentecost. Have you ever thought about how Jesus built His team?

Jesus was walking along the seashore when he saw two

young brothers, Simon and Andrew, throwing a net into the water as they fished. Jesus called out to them to follow Him, and they did. He then saw two other brothers, James and John, and invited them to also walk with Him. These men could have rejected Jesus' invitation because they were busy, they were assisting their families in business, or they had people they did not want to leave. They could have used several excuses that would have kept them from their season of growth, but they didn't.

Have you ever wondered about their friends who did not walk with them? Did they build their own fishing businesses or become tax collectors and just live life normally? We do know that those Jesus chose who accepted the call became apostles and became leaders in the New Testament church.

Either we grow together or we outgrow each other. Sometimes you grow apart and love those people who had been with you in your stuck season from a distance. You may have to move them from your VIP section to the balcony and love them from afar. You can walk in forgiveness without having to walk by their sides. At some point you must stop being available to those you have outgrown because their weight, whether mental, emotional, or physical, will stunt your own growth.

It's so easy to offer excuses for why we can't walk out our purpose while remaining in unhealthy relationships. We may have fallen in love with a person's potential instead of accepting that they may never live up to those standards. I often say that we fall in love with their charisma, but we have to live with their character. There are times when we keep certain people in our lives much longer than is necessary because we just can't stand change. Stop trying to give life to stagnant or dead relationships.

The sooner you detach yourself from anything or anyone no longer assisting you in growing emotionally, mentally, and physically, the sooner you will become the person of purpose God called you to be. Sometimes it's hard for us to leave certain people or situations in order to grow because we want them to succeed with us, but to go where we are destined to be, we may need to detach and move forward without them.

Situations in life are always changing, and characters in your life's story may also change. You are allowed to change relationships as you enter new seasons. Some friends cannot grow where you are going. Following are some signs that signal change is needed.

YOU NO LONGER HAVE ANYTHING IN COMMON

When you are together, you reiterate things of the past. It's as though you cannot agree on anything happening in this season. You have absolutely nothing to talk about when it comes to the now. As you are released from your stuckness, you realize your desires and interests have changed and you no longer enjoy talking about the good old days when you were in pain.

You are living your life for today and tomorrow and refuse to retrace actions that had broken you down. Yet, when you are with those in your life who cannot or will not grow, you feel stifled, manipulated, or even guilty that you are moving on. Just as there are seasons in nature—fall, winter, spring, and summer—we, too, have seasons in our lives.

Before God formed us, He knew we would face seasons of mistakes and end up feeling less than. He knew we would take ourselves off the couture rack and put ourselves on the clearance rack. But He also knew that our messes would become our message and our scars would turn into stars. When you realize that God has qualified you no matter what society tells you, you will then become that new person who has left that old season and refused to go back.

YOUR LIFE GOALS ARE DIFFERENT

You have determined life goals that you realize are nonnegotiable. You are making plans that involve a personal relationship with Jesus Christ. You realize that your greatest gift from God is today. You can wake up in the morning and know that His faithfulness is new every morning. You no longer walk out the judgment of those whom you used to allow to determine your happiness.

YOU NO LONGER WANT TO PICK UP YOUR OLD HABITS

When I began making changes, I determined I could no longer hang out after work with the same crowd. I had been the life of the party on girls nights at the bar. But what had that gotten me? I would arrive home, and my little boys would already be asleep. Their mommy wasn't there to tuck them in or read a bedtime story; she was partying with the girls.

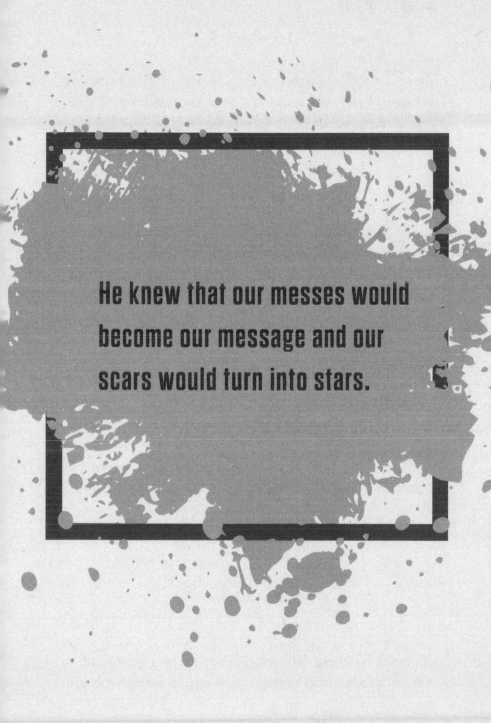

He knew that our messes would become our message and our scars would turn into stars.

———

There is a season when you get sick and tired of being the victim in your own story and you are ready for change. This is the moment when you quit expecting loved ones or friends to fix you and you decide it's time for you to do it yourself. It's as simple as the sinner's prayer—believe on the Lord Jesus Christ and be saved. It's that moment when you realize that you are the only one, with God's help, who can make change happen in your life. No one else can produce the results that will bring you happiness.

As I began walking through my new season, I finally understood the importance of growth. If you really want someone out of your life, that someone who had allowed you to stay stuck, then remove yourself.

It was not easy. There were times I would rather have stayed in a broken world than worked hard to make changes. It would have been easier to stay comfortable in my pain, my broken marriage, my failing business, and just settle. It felt easier to settle for less than God promised me. I realize now that God never left me while I was stuck in my pain. The Bible tells us that He never leaves us and never forsakes us:

> Don't love money; be satisfied with what you
> have. For God has said,
> "I will never fail you.
> I will never abandon you."
>
> (HEBREWS 13:5)

We don't always understand how or why we end up in certain seasons. Life happens. Sometimes it's the result of a decision or decisions we've made and we cannot imagine how to turn life around.

I think about the woman with the alabaster box. She *was* sinful, yes, but who she was and what she did will never be forgotten. As she entered the house of Simon, the Pharisee, to see Jesus, everyone in that room knew who she was. We know her as the woman with the alabaster box of sweet perfume, but everyone else knew her as the sinful woman. This woman was recognized by most men on the street.

> One of the Pharisees asked Jesus to have dinner with him, so Jesus went to his home and sat down to eat. When a certain immoral woman from that city heard he was eating there, she brought a beautiful alabaster jar filled with expensive perfume. Then she knelt behind him at his feet, weeping. Her tears fell on his feet, and she wiped them off with her hair. Then she kept kissing his feet and putting perfume on them. (Luke 7:36–38)

This woman heard that Jesus was having dinner in the home of the Pharisee, and she walked in carrying her alabaster box. The men who had been invited for dinner must have gasped as she walked through the door. How dare she, a lowly sinner, and a woman at that, enter their presence? But she had heard about the miracles Jesus had performed and that He did not discriminate between Jews and Gentiles like the rest of society did. He loved everyone, so she wanted to worship Him. She wanted His forgiveness.

All she had was an expensive bottle of perfume; people have estimated it to have been worth the equivalent of one year's salary. Entering that room and coming into Jesus' presence, she began weeping and knelt behind Him at His feet. She let down her hair and began drying His feet with her hair. *Scandalous!* I'm sure that was the group's thought. Why did this sinful woman with a bad reputation believe she was qualified to be in that room with those men, especially with Jesus? Who had given her permission to even be present when she had definitely not been invited? Simon, the Pharisee, said to himself, *If He were a prophet, He would know she was a sinner.*

This woman did not allow Simon or any other man to deter her from the desire to worship the Savior who could offer her the forgiveness she was seeking. She stood behind Jesus as Jesus stood between her and Simon. When we come to Jesus, He becomes the buffer for our pain. He stands between us and those who have critically judged us or refuse to love or forgive us—the ones who cannot allow our past to be forgotten. This woman did not hide in the corner.

When we come to Jesus, He becomes the buffer for our pain.

From the moment she walked into the Pharisee's home, she saw Simon's disdain. To Simon, she *was* her sin. She was the fruit of everything that she had done. Simon saw her full of sin and broken, but Jesus saw her humbly reaching out for forgiveness. She knew she was guilty of everything for which these men were judging her, but Jesus was standing in the gap for this lost soul.

"I tell you, her sins—and they are many—have been forgiven, so she has shown me much love. But a person who

is forgiven little shows only little love." Then Jesus said
to the woman, "Your sins are forgiven." (Luke 7:47–48)

Jesus knew the heart of this fallen woman and the very
cry of her soul. He knew she was ready for change and
would no longer allow her stuckness to rule her every decision. If you have ever felt rejected, betrayed, unwanted, and
unloved, then you understand how this woman determined
she would do whatever was necessary to find change, even
among those full of judgment. You may still hear the voices
of your past saying that you haven't changed, you've fallen
again, or you've failed your family another time. But I'm
telling you that Jesus sees your heart. He understands your
purpose is greater than your pain.

Growth means you get up one more time than you fall
down. Growth means you no longer allow the pain of the
past to determine your future. Your future is determined by
how you act today. You are defined
by what God says about you and
how you respond to that truth.

Growth means you get up one more time than you fall down.

The woman with the alabaster
box never should have entered the
house of the Pharisee, yet she did.
Her future was pulling her past into the present so she could
face her pain and see change. She did not have a tribe of
supporters as she entered that room of judgment. She stood
alone, accepting that she was a sinner and wanting to be
redeemed by this man called Jesus. This is how you grow.
You understand your future is full of possibilities. You will
no longer allow anyone or anything in your past to define you.

When people write you off, God writes you on. You will no longer fuel the fire by believing the chatter. You can be free; you can be healed. Paul let us know God's grace is sufficient for us. The disgrace of my past does not determine the inheritance of my future:

> Each time he said, "My grace is all you need. My power works best in weakness." So now I am glad to boast about my weaknesses, so that the power of Christ can work through me. (2 Corinthians 12:9)

On the worst of my days, I asked my mom how I could move on when so many people were judging me for my past. I understood that I was guilty of the charges. I had lived life out of control. But how do you begin a new life when people will not allow you to change? When your past reputation is bigger than life and people will not let your past be your past?

My mom rocked my world the day she said to me, "Kimberly, I lived many years afraid to change because of the whispers in the dark." Whoa! What did that mean? My mom had never rebelled against anyone. I always said that I did everything I did because my mom and dad would never understand the ways of the world. Someone in the family had to understand sinners, so, I guess that would be me.

As I mentioned in chapter 6, after they married, my parents joined a religious organization with many restrictions to assist them in defining holiness. For eighteen years our church had a reputation for its high standards. No makeup, no jewelry, no women wearing pants, no televisions, no cutting hair, dyeing hair, or wearing wigs. I remember when families left our church because the men had organized a church softball league. The elders determined that this was a form of reveling that was definitely a sin in the Bible.

When my mom and dad began to understand that God gave His only Son to die for our sins and that grace was God's gift, not something we earned, many people became restless and left the church. They could not engage in the freedom that was being given to them. They needed someone to orchestrate the boundaries of the church so they would feel certain about salvation. If they did not break the rules, then they would be elevated to heaven when they died.

My father preached that we could not work hard enough, dress holy enough, or live righteously enough to gain eternal life. Jesus went to the cross and carried our sins in His body so we could be made righteous. It took my mother one year to begin to accept this change and the importance of grace in salvation.

This was foreign to many of the families, not just my mom. What then was our responsibility as Christians? We were not to just accept the Lord as Savior and, by faith, live a life of compassion and love. Most believed works had to be involved in order to be saved.

Everything changed for my mom as she realized she no longer was expected to wear her long hair piled high on her head and that she could now wear jewelry and makeup. My mother's testimony is that she was born anew when she received this simple revelation about grace. She did not have to dress to please the pharisees of her day. She could spend time in communion and prayer with Jesus Christ and accept that He had made her righteous.

Her testimony thirty years later is that God gave her a new lease on life. She became intimately connected to Jesus Christ and now she looks younger and more beautiful than she did when she was thirty years old. She began a totally new personal relationship with Jesus Christ. One day while she was praying, she realized that when she passed and stood at judgment day with everyone who has ever lived on this earth, she would not be there as Mrs. Henry Jones, the wife of her husband, nor "the pastor's wife," nor her children's mother. She would represent herself and stand before God for everything that she, personally, had ever allowed or accomplished. This one revelation changed her life so much that the last thirty years have been as though she were a completely different person.

God accepts you and celebrates you even in your brokenness. You will inspire some and annoy others—do it anyway. Sometimes those broken people who walked by your side don't want you healed. We're all given the same opportunity to grow and change. It's simply up to us to take it and run with it. The people who choose to stay the same will end up left behind.

Life misfortunes that, in the past, took me out for years now are just speed bumps. I'm still not perfect, but all the people who prayed for my downfall can get their refund because Jesus loves to use the people with the worst pasts to create the best futures! *Boom shaka laka laka boom!*

GETTING UP!

DECLARATION

I once thought that losing people meant there was something wrong with me. Now I know that I am simply on the path to a new level of growth. I will not be moved by the people, places, and things that may fall off in this process. I will continue to get up and not quit, no matter how long it takes. I will use wisdom with the people in my life and set boundaries accordingly. I will no longer be moved by other people's opinions, and I will instead hold on to God's truths.

PRAYER

Jesus,
Thank You for giving me the opportunity to grow. I welcome the things You have in store for me that will shift me to my next level. Thank You for bringing the right people into my life at the right time. Help me turn the pain of change into purpose.
Amen.

PART IV
FREEDOM LOOKS GOOD ON YOU

You know when someone's life is in shambles. Look at any homeless person and you can immediately see the embarrassment, the pain of not knowing where their next meal is coming from. Then look at that person who just received a hefty promotion and the way they carry themselves. Look at that bride on her wedding day and then the same bride when she is leaving the lawyer's office after the divorce. There is a remarkable difference between freedom and pain. Won't you agree that freedom looks better on you?

RADICAL RESTORATION

I am a trauma survivor. From childhood trauma and adulthood trauma, I have survived only because of God. I was diagnosed with complex PTSD in 2018. Finally, I had a diagnosis. I had seen many therapists in my lifetime, but in 2020, my life changed for the better, and with no therapy this time!! I found Real Talk Kim's live videos and the rest is history! I was hooked from the very first video.

I had taken care of my brother with MS for twenty-three years. Even though his speech and cognitive function were affected from the MS, he totally understood Pastor Kim's sermons and would express his excitement by banging the arm of the chair as we watched her.

My brother contracted Covid-19 in 2021, and I lost him on Valentine's Day. In the months following his death, it was one attack after another. But I never lost hope or stopped watching Pastor Kim. She is what kept me going! I also joined the Inner Circle during this time!! That was another huge support for me. As I faced

some of the most difficult circumstances in my life, I still was the strongest I probably had ever been. Financially, I was in a major bind and my house was going to be foreclosed on. I never gave up on God. I sold my house and closed on the very day the bank was foreclosing. I moved to Fayetteville so I could be in Pastor Kim's church. I literally did what Bishop Kim teaches us. I mourned and moved! I am happy to say, I now own my own home and attend Limitless every Sunday. Life is good to say the least! Pastor Kim says, "If you have a pulse, God has a plan." I still had a pulse, so I knew my God had a plan for me! I am walking out His plan today.

—A

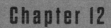

Chapter 12

GOD NEVER REVOKES HIS OFFER

Did you know that God will never reject you? He is always at work, and He always has a remnant chosen by grace to accomplish His will. When we feel alone, abandoned, or overwhelmed, we can know that our relationship with God is not based on our performance but simply upon our faith in Jesus Christ. He chose us before He created the world and predestined us to be His family.

Predestination means that God decided in advance to adopt us into His own family by bringing us to Himself through Jesus Christ. He chooses to love us and use us even when we don't deserve it. If it were anything else, it wouldn't be grace:

> Even before he made the world, God loved us and chose us in Christ to be holy and without fault in his eyes. (Ephesians 1:4)

Grace is the spontaneous, unmerited gift of divine favor in the salvation of sinners. Since the garden of Eden, we are born sinners. That doesn't change until we choose to believe in the Lord Jesus Christ, repent of our sins, and allow Jesus to be Lord of our lives.

Adam and Eve were chosen to be the guardians of the garden of Eden. They were blessed to be created by God simply for fellowship. God told them they could eat fruit from any of the trees in the garden except the tree of the knowledge of good and evil. They were warned that if they ate from that tree, they would die.

Adam and Eve failed the test. Eve was tempted by Satan and ate the fruit. She then gave the fruit to Adam. Eve was deceived, but Adam was not (1 Timothy 2:14). This did not lessen Adam's sin; it increased it because he sinned knowingly. Immediately, they knew they had sinned against God, became ashamed, and tried to hide their nakedness. Of course, there is no place on earth where we can hide from the almighty God.

Adam and Eve succumbed to sin in the garden of Eden, and God revoked their access to the most beautiful place on earth, but God did not abandon them, even though Adam and Eve were banished from the garden and could never again make it their home. However, they lived many years and had a family. Because we are their descendants, women will always have pain in childbearing and men will have to work for their food. It is a common joke among women as they deal with their monthly cycles that Eve is to blame for all their pain.

God may revoke His offer of opportunity if His people

fail in their stewardship of the tasks they have been given. There is a great danger in being stuck. It creates the loss of opportunity and place offered by Jesus. If they had passed this crucial test, death would not be as it is today. But because Adam failed as head of his household to protect his wife, God knew He must make a new plan. They were banished from the garden because of the consequences of sin and could not have the privilege of the tree of life any longer.

Please understand that God never revokes His offer for salvation, but He does revoke His offer of grace if we reject His offer of salvation. Is the offer still open even in our sin? Jesus said, "Unless you are born again, you cannot see the Kingdom of God" (John 3:3). Such a simple but profound statement that is true today. Yes, the offer of salvation is good even in our sin as we make a decision to step into the light and accept Him as Lord and Savior. Sometimes people reject Him; but it's never the Savior rejecting them:

> And since it is through God's kindness, then it is not by their good works. For in that case, God's grace would not be what it really is—free and undeserved. (Romans 11:6)

> "Teach these new disciples to obey all the commands I have given you. And be sure of this: I am with you always, even to the end of the age." (Matthew 28:20)

We can take great comfort in knowing God will never leave us nor forsake us. His grace is free and undeserved, and He will always be with us. When the first man, Adam, sinned, God's new plan was to send His only begotten Son,

Jesus Christ, to be born into an earthly family and live here thirty-three and one-half years. Then He would be offered up as a sacrifice for the sins of the world. This baby, who was both God and man, did not come as a king in a palace but as a newborn babe wrapped in swaddling clothes, lying in a manger, a feeding trough for animals.

ONE CHANCE, TWO CHANCES, THREE CHANCES, AND MORE

I am so thankful today that God gave me one chance, two chances, three chances, and more to submit myself to Him and offer my life up as a living sacrifice. Have I failed? More times than I can count. And yet, He has never forsaken me. Thank God He never revoked His offer of salvation. Because He continually reached out to me, I have now hugged thousands of people in face-to-face encounters that allow me to tell them how very precious they are to God and to me.

Mother Teresa wrote, "I don't think there is anyone who needs God's help and grace as much as I do." I understand why Mother Teresa could write such a statement. Sometimes I, too, feel as though I have failed God too many times. Then I fall into His arms of grace and mercy and realize that is why He uses me to carry His gospel to thousands weekly. I cannot depend on my own strength; I totally rely on Him, twenty-four hours a day, seven days a week. I understand that nothing can be revived in my life unless I own where I am.

The apostle Paul is a great example of a strong yet weak man who completely depended on God. He was one of the most influential leaders of the early church and started more than twelve churches while writing thirteen books of the Bible. Before Paul was known as a crusader for the sake of the gospel, he was known for persecuting Christians. He was a Pharisee like his father and went to the strictest schools for Jewish boys. Paul's identity was rooted in his Jewishness, but he had a once-in-a-lifetime, come-to-Jesus conversion while he was on the way to Damascus to persecute more Christians.

Because Paul was a Roman citizen, he had special privileges that probably saved him from abuse several times after his conversion. When he was converted, it upset everyone. He was being educated to eventually become a notable rabbi in the Jewish faith. Now this young man was telling everyone that they were not guaranteed a place in heaven just because they were born a Jew.

Paul was called by God to carry the gospel to the Gentiles. This man who had been taught Jewish customs from birth was teaching the Gentiles that they did not need to adopt Jewish customs. Even though Paul was associated with at least seven different miracles in the New Testament, he expressed his own dependence on the Holy Spirit when he wrote about his thorn in the flesh. He called it Satan's messenger sent to torment him.

> Even though I have received such wonderful revelations from God. So to keep me from becoming proud, I was given a thorn in my flesh, a messenger from Satan to torment me and keep me from becoming proud.
>
> Three different times I begged the Lord to take it away.

Each time he said, "My grace is all you need. My power works best in weakness." So now I am glad to boast about my weaknesses, so that the power of Christ can work through me. That's why I take pleasure in my weaknesses, and in the insults, hardships, persecutions, and troubles that I suffer for Christ. For when I am weak, then I am strong. (2 Corinthians 12:7–10)

We don't know what Paul's thorn in his flesh was. We do know that because he had received many revelations from God, this thorn came from Satan to keep Paul from being exalted in the eyes of the people. Many more people would have received Paul's teachings if they had seen him living a more comfortable life.

This messenger of Satan was always buffeting Paul to scare away the fainthearted. Paul pleaded with the Lord three times to take the thorn away. God let Paul know that His grace was sufficient and His power was made perfect in Paul's weakness. Are you relating to Paul in your season? Have you realized you, too, have a thorn in your flesh? I can tell you that God will prove sufficient for you as you face your challenges to become the crusader He called you to be.

If Paul, who had been a staunch activist in the Jewish faith, could become the greatest soul winner in the New Testament church, it sets the stage for you and me to determine that we are also part of God's bigger plan. God has deliberately put His treasure in fragile jars of clay like you and me and anyone else who chooses to allow the Holy Spirit to reside within them:

We now have this light shining in our hearts, but we ourselves are like fragile clay jars containing this great treasure. This makes it clear that our great power is from God, not from ourselves. (2 Corinthians 4:7)

FRAGILE JARS OF CLAY

We are all vulnerable, fragile jars of clay with unseen treasure inside. When you see me, you see only the outer shell, or house, that encompasses the spirit that is the true me. Our flesh is dying daily from the moment we draw our first breath until we are finished with this life. We're just the messengers with the greatest message of everlasting life.

Aren't you so thankful that God keeps forgiving and then forgetting our shortcomings? If you received your faith from someone who has now lost theirs or who is not where they once were with the gospel of Jesus Christ, understand that the message you received came to you through a fragile jar of clay. It isn't the jar that matters but the message you received. The treasure within us is the message of Jesus Christ given by God.

We carry this precious message around in the unadorned clay pots of our ordinary lives to prevent anyone from confusing God's incomparable power with our own strength. Although the jars are wasting away, and on the outside it looks like things are falling apart, not a day goes by without His amazing grace.

I realize that no matter how well we take care of our bodies, we will one day succumb to death and go to our

We carry this precious message around in the unadorned clay pots of our ordinary lives to prevent anyone from confusing God's incomparable power with our own strength.

forever home. No matter how much we invest in our health and beauty, we will all leave this earth one day. Collagen injections, Botox, liposuction, and face-lifts are only temporary fixes for these fragile jars of clay with permanent destinations.

> That is why we never give up. Though our bodies are dying, our spirits are being renewed every day. For our present troubles are small and won't last very long. Yet they produce for us a glory that vastly outweighs them and will last forever! (2 Corinthians 4:16–17)

When we think we are waiting on God, He is waiting on us. Even when we keep failing and seem to sabotage the next season, He wants us to remember that He never revokes His offer. We are called and chosen for this season. So, it's time to move. Even if we have only one piece of the puzzle, move.

As we move, the pieces will begin to fall into place. I know this because God doesn't wreck His reputation on any of us. I am a poster child for failing at getting ahead of God. That is why, in my fiftieth year on this earth, I determined to seek His will before I make decisions in my ministry and especially in my personal life.

> "I knew you before I formed you in your
>   mother's womb.
>   Before you were born I set you apart
>   and appointed you as my prophet to the
>   nations." (Jeremiah 1:5)

Jeremiah was the "weeping prophet" who pronounced God's judgment on the people of his time for their wickedness. In his day, he was known as a prophet who could hear the voice of God. When God called Jeremiah, he was barely twenty years old and had no confidence that he was qualified to prophesy as God instructed. Jeremiah lacked confidence because of his youth, but God encouraged him by saying, "Don't be afraid of the people, for I will be with you and will protect you" (1:8). In the coming years, Jeremiah faithfully prophesied whenever God spoke a word.

Jeremiah was but a fragile jar of clay, a young man uncertain of his purpose when God called him. Thank God he obeyed when called. You've probably heard the saying "Face the fear and do it anyway." That's exactly what Jeremiah did. He did not allow fear to detour him from his destiny.

When you truly realize that you, too, have been called by God for a certain purpose, you will do whatever is necessary to fulfill that purpose. The day God created you, He was excitedly forming every part of your being—your dominant nose, your five-finger forehead just like your daddy's, your brows, cheeks, and hair.

MY SEASON OF CHANGE

I was in a season of starting over when I was hired by the local Belk department store. I had lived out the labels that I had been given for so long that I felt I was blessed to have a job in retail. Even though I had owned a successful home interior business before my marriage failure, I did not believe I was capable of anything more. In that season, I was a fragile jar of clay. What else could happen?

And then there came that fateful day when I was fired from the Belk department store. *Was this a joke?* It became very real and not at all funny when the manager escorted me out of the store and told me that I was accused of time clock fraud. Several times it seemed I had failed to punch out when I went on break.

Those indiscretions came back to haunt me when I was being escorted to my car in disbelief. I thought I was getting a promotion when my name was called out over the sound system. Everyone knew I was being called to the manager's office. *Did everyone know that I was being fired?* That was what I thought about as I drove home.

When I arrived back at my mom's, I was devastated and embarrassed. How could I support my boys when I could not even keep a job? I had already lost our home, my business, my marriage, and now I had lost another job.

As I fell on the couch inconsolable, my mom let me know I could not remain there for long. If I had found the Belk job, I could find another job, and God would help me. She told me I had only a small window of time to mourn and then I needed to get moving. Time and life were marching on.

Two hours later when the phone rang, I was so depressed I did not want to talk to anyone. I wanted to detach from life as I had done before I was hired at the job that I thought was my saving grace. Mom handed me the phone and told me to answer it. Thank God I answered the phone that day. It was a lady from Bloomingdale's department store in a prestigious mall across town who was offering me a position in their fabulous store.

She could not offer me this position when I worked at Belk because I was already working in the same makeup line. When she heard I had been fired, she immediately called and hired me. It was unbelievable how quickly my life went from devastation to fulfillment. I was not only hired but received a hefty increase in salary.

God will use your mess for your next message.

This was God's grace in place. God will use your mess for your next message. Your devastation is working for your destiny. Even today, ten years later, I still refer to that season of being rescued and vindicated as my Bloomingdale's season!

I learned to be diligent in consistency during this season because I no longer took the time clock for granted. I was overzealous at being on time. Even when God was promoting me from the broken clay jar filled with pain and rejection to a hope dealer loving on people, I still held my position at Bloomingdale's.

I receive testimonies on a regular basis from fellow employees during that season who watched me transform from the inside out. I would clock out at lunch, walk to my car, and go live online with a prayer call as thousands joined. I remember the day I finished that prayer call, got out of my car, and looked around the parking garage as numerous employees were returning to work. I realized they had been with me on my prayer call.

I am a fragile jar of clay in the earthly body that God

formed purposefully and my parents named Kimberly. Many times I have been caught up in my own ego and it has sabotaged my future. However, now I know that God would not have had me walk through the pain of rejection and betrayal if He had not wanted to give me deliverance and destiny over my own dignity.

My life is full of thanksgiving to a Savior who would give me more chances than I deserve, bless me in more ways than I can imagine, and fulfill my life by filling it with love and compassion.

Things I have learned on this journey:

- God will never revoke His offer.
- It's important to know His character.
- Sometimes we need to just listen.
- If you don't have clear direction, keep doing what you do know to do.
- Your life will expand according to your courage.
- To get to your next level, your character will be tested.

GETTING UP!

DECLARATION

I once thought that I could never measure up. Now I know that God qualified me before I was even born. I declare that the treasure placed inside me will no longer be hidden. I have been adopted into the family of God by grace through faith. God's offer of salvation will never be revoked, and I will walk in the authority that was given to me through Jesus. I will move in integrity so that my character will keep up with my purpose.

PRAYER

Jesus,
Thank You for my salvation that You paid for on the cross. Thank You for choosing me and always being at work in my life. Help me to become completely dependent on You alone. Show me how to become consistent and how to work with You every day.
Amen.

RADICAL RESTORATION

I started listening to RTK in 2018 after she ministered at my church. I was lost and stuck! I was saved at twenty-two years old. After we married, my husband and I served at our church, and we later became youth leaders. After years of serving at our church, our marriage failed. I stopped going to church and divorced my husband. I was backslidden and reckless for eight years while my ex-husband continually prayed that God would return my heart to Jesus! It worked! God is faithful! But I was stuck and struggling.

The only one who could reach my soul (my mind, my will, my emotions) and cause my spirit to seek God again was Pastor Kim! I remember listening to her and Mimi while she was in a hotel room, and she said that you must forgive to be released! In the chat, I told Pastor Kim that I felt stuck because I had unforgiveness toward my former youth pastors. I prayed for the first time to forgive them! I knew I was set free. I honestly know that when I forgave, God forgave me of my sin! I am free today because Pastor Kim would say to get up, get up out of this funk! You can do it, you can be free! You can have freedom!!!

Being connected to those who have walked through the church shame, the guilt, the hurt, the forgiveness makes a difference in your life! I was stuck for twenty years!!! Within four years of listening to RTK, I am free!!! I'm sure it would've been sooner if I was faithfully plugged in, but I had layers that I had to peel through! Jesus is so good and knew I needed Pastor Kim. Thank you, Pastor Kim! I can't wait for you to see your rewards in heaven. My life was changed because you had the boldness to share your pain, and I was able to work through mine!

—R

Chapter 13

LET IT GO

Did you know that airport employees are trained to carefully calculate how much baggage a plane can carry? You may have experienced added fees they assess to discourage you from packing too much. Overloading a plane will affect the plane's performance and the integrity of its overall structure. It doesn't just affect the pilot and the crew; it puts everyone in danger. This is the same principle in our own lives when it comes to carrying around unnecessary baggage.

Unnecessary baggage can be made up of the emotional hurts we've never dealt with, regrets, betrayals, you name it. It takes intentionality to live free of the baggage that would try to weigh us down and keep us from reaching God's destination for us.

Here are two steps to help you live free of the baggage:

- Realize that God may expose things or even relationships that you need to release, not to hurt you but to expand you and take you higher. We can expand our ability to heal.
- Recognize that some people leaving your life is a blessing because rejection is God's protection! It's not personal, it's spiritual!

You might be wondering what extra weight you are carrying around. How would you even know?

Sometimes we get so used to carrying around pain, rejection, and betrayal that we no longer feel their weight. Sometimes you don't realize how toxic the air is until the toxic things leave and you are breathing easily. Many people have lost their lives breathing in carbon monoxide, a deadly gas that is colorless and does not smell. You might only sense you were in trouble if you experienced a headache. That is why there are carbon monoxide detectors for our homes today.

Likewise, it's important for you to have *spiritual* detectors that sense the pain you are carrying, allowing it to weigh you down, to hold you back from your purpose, and to hide God's voice. I have learned on my journey of freedom to allow the Holy Spirit to be my spiritual barometer in measuring my levels of distrust and pain that had become so familiar that I did not realize they were distracting me from my destiny.

Sometimes you do not realize you still carry the baggage

until you attempt to enter a new relationship, personal or professional. That's when it's time to seek help from godly counselors, Christian friends, the Word of God, and prayer. Why attempt something brand-new when you are the same broken person inside with a new façade? Trying to move on when you have not consciously let go of the past and walked in forgiveness. It's worth your time and effort to make the change.

When flying, if a pilot is off course only one little degree for sixty miles, the plane will miss its targeted destination by one mile. What's your one degree? What baggage have you picked up throughout your life's journey that is determining you will end up at a misguided destination?

You can improve your life today by consciously seeing yourself on the other side of your pain, your rejection, and your betrayal, and by not allowing a season in your life to define your lifetime, not allowing it to detour the whole plane. Let's take a look at some of the unnecessary, hindering baggage you may need to release.

UNNECESSARY, HINDERING BAGGAGE

Regret

We cannot allow our past failures to define our futures or we will never reach the heights and depths God has for us. Whatever we do with the pain of the past determines who we become. Who we become affects how we walk out our lives! Scars are evidence of overcoming; scars do not equal failure! If we're always looking back, we'll never be able to see what's ahead. Remember Lot's wife, whom we discussed in chapter 2? She became permanently stuck in her past because she could not keep her eyes on what God had for her future.

> "But forget all that—
>> it is nothing compared to what I am going
>>> to do.
> For I am about to do something new.
>> See, I have already begun! Do you not
>>> see it?
> I will make a pathway through the wilderness.
>> I will create rivers in the dry wasteland."
>
> (ISAIAH 43:18–19)

Stop and think about it. Does regret change anything? Nope. Will regret give you an opportunity to go back and fix it? Nope. Why do we spend so much time and get so stuck on feelings of regret when it's impossible to rewind time and have a redo? You gotta get up! Choose to shift your perspective and let go of the regrets. It happened! It's done! It's time to let go. Turn your regrets into wisdom and keep on moving.

Fear

Many of us are called to break barriers and do things that no one in our family or immediate circle has ever done. Could you be the key to changing the trajectory of your whole family? Know that fear can only keep you from moving forward if you allow it to. Fear has no power over you unless you give it power.

When Jesus died on the cross, He handed over all authority to us so that we could be more than conquerors. Everything and everyone must bow at the name of Jesus, and that includes fear! If you don't deal with the fear, you'll never reach what God has for you. You'll stay where you are right now for the rest of your life. Choose to break the cycle!

> For God has not given us a spirit of fear and timidity, but of power, love, and self-discipline. (2 Timothy 1:7)

Too often we allow our minds to become plagued with the what-if questions.

What if it doesn't work?
What if I fall after stepping out?
What if it doesn't turn out how I wanted it to?

At some point, you have to quit asking all the questions and just start doing. You gotta get up! Take a step and do it afraid, do it with your knees knocking! Remember that failure isn't failure unless you don't get back up. A "failure" is just proof that you are trying, you are moving, you are putting feet to your faith and doing something.

Remember that failure isn't failure unless you don't get back up.

Look at failure as a part of your success story. You don't even have to take a huge leap right out of the gate. Even just one small step is still a step forward in the right direction. Fear will try to paralyze you, but we've been given the power to overcome!

Unwillingness to Change

Stepping into something new will always require us to do something new. Change requires us to change. We cannot expect a different result if we are unwilling to do things differently. God will show us changes that need to be made in order for us to walk victoriously through life.

Sometimes it's a character issue, sometimes it's a mindset issue, sometimes it's a habit that needs to be broken or a box that you need to step out of. Stop and ask yourself, *Can my character keep up with my calling?* Are you willing to do whatever God asks of you to reach that next level? How flexible are you?

Second Timothy 4:2 says, "Be prepared, whether the time is favorable or not." Sometimes God wants to shake us up in order to change our path and change our season. But He is also a gentleman and will never force us to do anything we don't want to do. As humans, we get so used to our routines and the things we do on a daily basis. Sometimes we simply get stuck in the routine.

In order to truly move forward, we have to be willing and open to change, whatever that may look like. Not all change is going to look like fun or feel good. They're not called "growing pains" for no reason, right?

———

Queen Esther is one of the greatest examples of embracing change. She shifted her entire life. She left her home and family for an opportunity to become royalty even though this was not an easy feat. Esther, a Jew, had been raised by her older cousin Mordecai. When Mordecai heard that a new queen would be chosen, he sent Esther to Hegai, who was in charge of preparing the young women to meet the king. Esther's beauty and spirit won her special attention with Hegai, and Esther became the new queen.

Not long after becoming queen, Esther discovered an evil plot to annihilate her people. God had shaken up her life and sent her to the king's palace "for such a time as this." Mordecai told her she must go before the king and beg for the lives of their people even though it was against the law to go to the king without first being summoned.

Esther had a choice, and she chose to do the uncomfortable thing. Because of this, Queen Esther saved not only her own life but also her whole nation.

Comparison

Comparison is one of the biggest hindrances to walking freely in who God created us to be. When we get caught up comparing our lives and our purposes to other people's, we lose sight of what God has for us. We each have a unique call on our life; we each were made with a specific purpose. God didn't mass-produce humans; He created us individually. Yet we waste so much time trying to be like one another.

Think of your life as a seed. If you're so busy comparing yourself to everyone else instead of nurturing what God gave you, your efforts will yield no fruit. You can't produce what you were never given the seed for! In other words, you have to stop trying to act like someone else.

Comparison is a tool the enemy uses to keep us distracted

because he knows there is power in who God created us to be! No one can do things the way that you can do things. People might be able to steal your recipe, but they'll never be able to duplicate your sauce. Do you! Be you! There is nothing that compares to true authenticity.

Unforgiveness

Unforgiveness is like poison to the soul. It will spread and contaminate the healthy parts of you if it's not dealt with. When you hold on to unforgiveness, you will bleed on people who didn't cut you. It will affect all the people who are called to walk alongside you. Don't believe the lie that unforgiveness can be "managed" or "contained." You may not notice it right away, but eventually, unforgiveness will begin to manage you!

> Look after each other so that none of you fails to receive the grace of God. Watch out that no poisonous root of bitterness grows up to trouble you, corrupting many. (Hebrews 12:15)

When we allow bitterness to get into our hearts, it's comparable to when a plant gets root rot. The plant becomes useless! The rot that starts only at the root will eventually spread throughout the whole plant. This is the same way unforgiveness works in our lives. It will spread into our words, our actions, our perspectives, until everything we do is tainted by unforgiveness.

Being a Christian does not promise a perfect life. We all go through heartbreaks, betrayals, and losses. We can choose how we will allow these things to affect us. The hurt may not have been your fault, but the healing is your responsibility.

Don't let your God-given potential be buried under the different baggage life will throw your way. Baggage isn't baggage until you choose to carry it. Who wants extra weight holding you down when you're trying to forge a new path? It's time to unpack the bags and let God deal with what you've been carrying. The baggage is a blockage. Once you begin to let go, you will find new things being awakened in you:

> No, dear brothers and sisters, I have not achieved it, but I focus on this one thing: Forgetting the past and looking forward to what lies ahead, I press on to reach the end of the race and receive the heavenly prize for which God, through Christ Jesus, is calling us. (Philippians 3:13–14)

The apostle Paul was speaking to the Christians in Philippi when he gave them a personal glimpse into his own understanding of walking with Christ. He knew he must focus on the present and future and intentionally disregard his past so that it did not keep him from moving forward. He let us know that, to reach the end of our life journey with confidence that we would obtain our promise in the heavenly realm, we, too, could not continually carry regret, unwillingness to change, comparison, and unforgiveness. So, let it go!

GETTING UP!

DECLARATION

I once thought it was my right to hold on to the things that hurt me. Now I am no longer afraid of letting go. I release all the baggage that has been weighing me down. I let go of all regret, fear, my unwillingness to change, comparison, and unforgiveness. I will no longer pick up any baggage that does not belong to me! My spiritual detectors are working perfectly, and I will heed the warnings of the Holy Spirit.

PRAYER

Jesus,
Thank You for being the Pilot of my life. I give you permission to direct the proper loading and unloading of my spiritual plane. Help me to know what to pick up and what to put down. Show me how to stay free from the things targeted to weigh me down.
Amen.

RADICAL RESTORATION

When I say God is amazing, He truly is. I am the mother of four amazing children, three girls and one boy. I work full time and have my associate of arts degree in business administration. In 2013, my now ex-husband cheated on me with a minor, a fifteen-year-old, and they had a child. At the time, I was pregnant with our son. This time in my life was the absolute worst. I contemplated committing suicide for seven months, but what stopped me was coming across Real Talk Kim's post. I was immediately inspired. I stayed with my ex-husband for a while because I allowed people to influence me. He was never convicted of this crime. Nine years later, I tried to make our relationship work again. This time, my ex had an affair with someone in our church and left with her. Today, I am happily divorced and in a wonderful relationship with an awesome man. Love after divorce is hard but amazing. Also, the podcast episode about "Blended Families" by Real Talk Kim was right on time. Thank you so much.

—L

Chapter 14

JUST ONE STEP

Now's the time to do the work. You've read up to this point and are hopefully inspired to make some changes in your life. I'm happy to share this part of my journey with you. But prepare yourself. You will need to take in this chapter slowly and allow the time to process. It is hard work to go deep, but oh, so worth it! You may find it helpful to dedicate a journal to use as you work through this chapter.

First, it's important to identify your purpose. Then I'll share more about the steps I took that changed my life.

YOUR PURPOSE

Everything we do in life has a purpose. We eat because our bodies need fuel. We drink water because our bodies need hydration. It's all to stay alive. It's the same with God. There are no accidents with Him. There is nothing coincidental. Everything has a purpose. He sees the bigger picture when we only see one step ahead.

God wants you to know your purpose. Misery comes when we live our lives aimlessly.

> Take delight in the LORD,
>   and he will give you your heart's desires.
> Commit everything you do to the LORD.
>   Trust him, and he will help you.
>
> (PSALM 37:4–5)

Too often we take verse 4 and forget about verse 5, which tells us to commit our ways to the Lord. Finding your true purpose takes surrender. When we "commit our way" to constant collaboration with God, He will show us our true desires. You may find, as you begin your purpose journey, that you desire one thing. But as you deepen your relationship with God, new desires will be awakened. Be open to the things God is revealing to you—you might be surprised.

Create Your Purpose Statement

Even though each one of us has a unique purpose, it is still not about us! It's all about serving—serving God and serving others. One of the most important actions you can take on your journey to freedom is to create your own purpose statement to help you understand why you were created. A strong purpose statement sets a path for how you will move forward, which will help you set clear goals.

As we journey through life, our first duty is to get free so we can then do the will of the Father. When Jesus was asked about the greatest commandment, He replied,

> "'You must love the LORD your God with all your heart, all your soul, and all your mind.' This is the first and greatest commandment. A second is equally important: 'Love your neighbor as yourself.'" (Matthew 22:37–39)

Remember, you cannot love others until you learn to love yourself.

Loving Others

Start your purpose statement like this: I, _____, was created with purpose to bring glory to God. I exalt God by loving others as He instructed in His Word.

When Jesus was on the earth, He truly loved His disciples and even knelt and washed their feet (John 13:12–17). Jesus, the Son of God, came to this earth and did nothing for Himself. Everything He did was out of love for the people around Him and for all of us. When He was in the garden of Gethsemane, He asked God if there were any other way than for Him to be crucified, yet He still said, "Your will be done." Jesus promised we will be blessed as we love others, as He Himself demonstrated.

Serving Others

Now, add to your statement: I, _____, was created with purpose to bring glory to God. I exalt God in my life by loving others *and serving them* as He instructed in His Word.

A great example of surrender and serving with purpose was Queen Esther. Remember her story from chapter 13? She chose to surrender and serve as she was purposed to do. For every powerful story in the Bible, there was a person who surrendered their life and chose to serve.

Moses was in the wilderness tending his father-in-law's animals when God asked him to lead the Israelites out of Egypt into the promised land. Moses consented, returned to his home country, and led the children of Israel out of slavery.

David had a heart of surrender. He started out as a shepherd boy, served King Saul, and became the greatest king of Israel.

Joseph kept his heart right through years of injustice, served wherever he was placed, and was able to bless those who plotted his demise. After Joseph interpreted Pharaoh's dreams, Pharaoh put Joseph in charge of the entire land of Egypt, removed his signet ring from his hand, and placed it on Joseph's finger. Joseph became second-in-command to Pharaoh as prime minister of Egypt.

There are no limits with God. The greater the surrender, the greater the purpose that is completed.

Your Life Verb

I, _____, was created with purpose to bring glory to God. I exalt God in my life by loving others, serving others as He instructed in His Word, and by_____ them.

We are all called to love and serve. What is the third thing that you are uniquely designed to do? I call that your "life verb." Once you figure it out, you can complete your purpose statement.

Need some inspiration? Here are mine:

- I, Kimberly Jones, was created with purpose to bring glory to God. I exalt God in my life by loving others, serving others as He instructed in His Word, and by *encouraging* (motivational speaker, pastor, teacher) those I meet daily.
- I, Kimberly Jones, was created with purpose to bring glory to God. I exalt God in my life by loving others, serving others as He instructed in His Word, and by *connecting* them (networking, facilitating divine connections).
- I, Kimberly Jones, was created with purpose to bring glory to God. I exalt God in my life by loving others, serving others as He instructed in His Word, and by *educating* them (teacher, life coach).

What is your life verb? If you are unsure, think about how others describe you. What are you known for? Are you a problem solver, organizer, motivator, encourager? Most important, ask God what one word describes you. Even one word of direction can shift your trajectory. Remember, this is only an example to assist you in getting that direction needed to identify your purpose.

This purpose statement will probably look a lot different by the time you complete it.

- Start out with something general, then allow God to fine-tune it. He will assist you in tailoring it to your own specifications.
- Having a purpose statement for your life will help you

make better decisions. The "now you" will be able to make a decision that will accelerate the "future you."
- You will be able to live a more meaningful life with intentionality.

Cultivating a heart posture of surrender and living in service of others will put you in the right position for God to reveal your unique purpose. Even if you believe you already know your purpose, write out a purpose statement. Watch yourself become more focused than ever before. God will meet you where you are. You are getting up. You will no longer allow your decisions and actions to deter you from your bigger life purpose! You've got this! You are a life changer! Now, walk it out!

―――

I remember the day I made up my mind that I had no choice but to change. As a result of poor life decisions, the life I had envisioned never became my reality. It was as though I was always on the precipice of making things happen and yet the results were always disappointing. Are you relating to my journey? You're already one step ahead since you've identified your purpose.

ASK GOD TO HELP YOU

My first step was asking God for assistance. I finally realized that, while I had allowed Jesus to be my Savior, I was still trying to be independent and prove my worth. I'm sure my lack of self-esteem from feeling I never measured up to my friends or to my brother's scholastic averages, and from being labeled "learning disabled" throughout school, had attributed to my need to prove my worth.

But once I hit rock bottom, what could I lose? I had already lost a marriage, home, and business. I decided to give God a chance and let Him be the Lord and Savior that my parents had taught me He could be.

I realized that if I was stuck with no direction, there were others who also could be stuck in their pain, rejection, and sickness. They might need help. Our charge is to figure out the pivots we can make to get out of our stuckness and be released into our purpose. Consistently asking God for guidance and then making good decisions is arguably the most important habit you could ever develop.

REPLACE YOUR CLUTTERED MINDSET

Building better thinking, better habits, and a better life requires you to replace your cluttered mindset. It's amazing how imprisoned we can become as we fight the never-ending dialogue within us telling us there is no way out. It's easier to stay stuck than to fight that inner dialogue. I receive messages every day from people asking for help in breaking out of their old mindset to become a new creation. Following are a few changes you can make to begin to change your mindset. You can quit

- blaming others when you fall,
- allowing others to determine your direction,
- making excuses, and
- refusing to listen to good advice.

IDENTIFY ONE SIMPLE DECISION
YOU CAN MAKE TODAY

Stop allowing the process of making big changes to over-whelm you. Instead, identify the power of one simple decision you can make today.

When I began learning vocabulary words in elementary school, there were ten spelling words I needed to memorize for the test each Friday. We were building a foundation we would lean on for a lifetime. They were simple words, but I'm still using those vocabulary words in my conversations today.

When we are trying to make life changes, we must go back to the basics as we did in elementary school. Thoughtfully and prayerfully consider the following questions:

- What life situation did you allow to get you to what seems like the point of no return?
- What sent you over the edge of sanity and directed you to failure instead of success?
- What decision created a rift in your relationships that has not been repaired?

Then ask yourself the following questions and identify a decision you can make today:

- What is one thing you are willing to do to fix your marriage, other relationships, your finances, and so forth?
- What is one thing you can do to establish better communication with your child or other family members?
- What is one thing you can do to become more understanding of your parents?

IS THIS AS GOOD AS IT'S GOING TO GET?

Once you've made your decision, you'll need to develop habits that will lead to better living.

Identify the power of "one decision": Start somewhere! Counseling is great; however, change is still going to depend on you. *You* gotta get up! Take your first step and then develop consistency in decision-making.

List changes that you can make to set you up for your new journey. You can choose one at a time to prepare yourself for your new you.

1. Scroll your social media accounts, delete anyone whom you understand is causing you pain, and unfollow those you sense are sabotaging your future.
2. Take a closer look at your friends and prayerfully consider taking a break from those who continually stir up drama. It's time to allow peace to rule.
3. Choose new hangouts. Give yourself an opportunity to grow by enlarging your sphere of influence.

4. Carefully scrutinize those friends who have become too comfortable with you. They have allowed themselves to walk in judgment without realizing the pain that has occurred.

5. If married, determine that you will no longer walk in unforgiveness. Take time for introspection. Seek out other couples who can assist you in releasing the pain of the past to begin a new journey. Make sure you begin this journey together or work on yourself until you two can walk in harmony together.

6. If divorced, decide you will no longer allow your mistakes to define you. Begin a journey of release: look within at changes that need to be made so you will not repeat the same mistakes that helped break you.

7. It's time for a whole new look. Allow new influencers to make a difference in your daily walk. New hairstyle, new wardrobe (one outfit at a time).

8. Begin researching influencers who will assist you in turning over a new leaf. Listen to podcasts, read books, or follow ministry leaders who relate to where you want to go.

9. Begin an exercise program that will help you become physically fit.

Additional Thoughts for Your New Journey

- **You know your heart's desires, so delete anything that is defeating you.** Sometimes you need to move those who are causing you pain from your VIP section to the balcony of your life.

- **You don't need to hang out with those who belittle you or go to places where they hang out.** Why allow others' actions to determine your altitude and attitude? Begin to trust your instincts again and realize that God gives us discernment to help us do the right thing. Have you ever made a bad judgment call and felt like your heart would beat out of your chest? Sometimes this could be the Holy Spirit allowing you to understand you messed up. You gotta get up, change your course, ask for forgiveness if necessary, and keep moving forward.
- **Recognize that physical and emotional abuse is not your life sentence.** I can tell you that I lived most of my life trying to prove that those who had warned me against certain relationships had no idea what they were talking about. My entire life was spent in recovery mode.

SUCCESS IS GETTING BACK UP

What do you do when you get off track? Success is getting up one more time than you fall down. We all have messed up many times. I have failed so many times that I cannot even recollect them all; however, I have gotten up one more time than I fell down. I am so thankful that I remember my failures so I can remember it's not me who got me to the position in life that I am enjoying today. It was totally God working through me, despite me. So, get up again and again, and take every failure as a life lesson on what not to do next time.

HAS THE HEALING PROCESS BEEN SUCCESSFUL?

Do you wake up each day excited about your next venture? Do you live in appreciation for God and for those who were there when you needed them? When you can face challenges and stay on your feet while your world is rocking, you learn that you were never promised a life without pain. You were only promised that God would never leave you nor forsake you.

GETTING UP!

DECLARATION

I once thought I would always live with unforgiveness and shame toward those in my life who have abused me. I now know that I can walk in freedom by forgiving those who have done me wrong. I can see the part I played in the situation, and I forgive myself for allowing unholy shame to dictate my life. I am not forgiving those who wronged me because they have asked but because it sets me free to be the me God created me to be.

PRAYER

Jesus,

As I begin my journey of release, give me insight into my responsibilities in becoming free. Assist me in forgiving those who have wounded or abused me. Allow me to see the reason for the rejection, the betrayal. Help me understand how to take the new free me and become responsible in loving and serving others as You demonstrated. I shall use this new season to change my world. Amen.

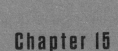

Chapter 15

A FINAL NOTE

Thank you for taking this journey with me. I hope you have found the inspiration you need to determine that you will not allow any situation to keep you stuck any longer. I trust you now know that you are not alone. Not only is Jesus Christ your Lord and Savior but there are also thousands reading along with you who are making the same life decisions that will change their focus for a lifetime.

When the reality that Jesus Christ died for me penetrated my being, I was able to honestly say, "Lord, I believe. I believe that You went to the cross for me, that You represented me on that cross, that You were buried and then resurrected on the third day so I could have eternal life and have it more abundantly." I am a walking and talking testimony that in a moment everything in my life changed.

> This means that anyone who belongs to Christ has become a new person. The old life is gone; a new life has begun! (2 Corinthians 5:17)

I can testify that salvation is instant and constant. We are instantly saved the moment we believe, and we are constantly saved as we let go of the old life and live in the new.

If you have not yet accepted Jesus as your Lord and Savior, there is no better time. It doesn't matter where you are or what you are doing, just take a moment and pray this prayer with me:

> *Jesus,*
> *I believe that You are my Savior. I believe that You died for me and rose from the grave and are now sitting at the right hand of the Father, interceding for me. I ask You to forgive me of my sins, come into my heart to stay, and change me from the inside out. Your Word tells me, "If we confess our sins, He is faithful and just to forgive us our sins and to cleanse us from all wickedness." Thank you for salvation, for the chance to live a new life in Christ. I now call you Lord because I accept You as my Lord and Savior, Jesus Christ.*

You have now begun a new life as a child of God. It's important for you to find a church community and join their family. You have stepped into the first day of the rest of your life!

ACCOUNTABILITY

It's essential that you have accountability in your journey of freedom to friends who will honestly assist you in moving forward toward your next season. Remember that your friends prophesy your future.

Look at your five closest friends today and consider how they face their difficult seasons. Are they negative or positive? Do they speak into their lives the truth from God's Word? Do they forgive and move on?

Your friends prophesy your future.

As I was walking into a dark storm, not knowing that I would be losing my husband and my dad within three months—my husband to divorce and my dad to the grave—the Lord nudged me to begin a mentoring group called the RTK Inner Circle. We have seen several thousand men and women join this accountability group and grow exponentially because they are receiving direction on how to forgive, to let it go, and to move on.

I had no idea I would need this group as much as they needed me. We embraced the idea of family, and we now celebrate the highs and lows of life together while growing in our spiritual lives. Everybody needs accountability. We cannot grow if we do not allow those placed in our lives for accountability to speak truthfully to us when we need it.

GOD'S WORD

Now that you have begun your new way of thinking and living, you need to get God's Word inside you daily so you can remain strong in the faith. I could not finish this journey with you without giving you some of my favorite scriptures that have become a mainstay in my life. Read these again and again until you memorize them so you can use them in all seasons of your new life. When you are feeling alone, quote His Word. When you need wisdom, ask Him for it. The Bible is full of promises. However, you won't know them unless you get into the Word.

My Favorite Verses

"Yes indeed, it won't be long now." GOD's Decree. "Things are going to happen so fast your head will swim, one thing fast on the heels of the other. You won't be able to keep up. Everything will be happening at once—and everywhere you look, blessings!" (Amos 9:13–15 THE MESSAGE)

"No weapon formed against you shall prosper,
And every tongue which rises against you in
    judgment
You shall condemn.
This is the heritage of the servants of
    the LORD,
And their righteousness is from Me,"
Says the LORD.

(ISAIAH 54:17 NKJV)

Death and life are in the power of the tongue,
And those who love it will eat its fruit.

(PROVERBS 18:21 NKJV)

The steps of a good man are ordered by the LORD,
And He delights in his way.

(PSALM 37:23 NKJV)

Blessed is the man
Who walks not in the counsel of the ungodly,
Nor stands in the path of sinners,
Nor sits in the seat of the scornful;
But his delight is in the law of the LORD,
And in His law he meditates day and night.
He shall be like a tree
Planted by the rivers of water,
That brings forth its fruit in its season,
Whose leaf also shall not wither;
And whatever he does shall prosper.

(PSALM 1:1–3 NKJV)

I can do all things through Christ who strengthens me.
(Philippians 4:13 NKJV)

For God has not given us a spirit of fear, but of power and
of love and of a sound mind. (2 Timothy 1:7 NKJV)

"For I know the plans I have for you," says the LORD.
"They are plans for good and not for disaster, to give you
a future and a hope." (Jeremiah 29:11)

There will be days that you will feel like you cannot move another step. You may feel like a turtle stuck in peanut butter, but you just keep moving. One of the greatest revelations of my family's life during our seasons of loss was to "mourn and move." You have a season you can mourn your loss, but then you must get up and move on because seasons are temporary. You can do it. You were created by God to have everything necessary to walk out your God-given purpose. I believe in you!

I'm constantly online and sending notifications to all who have downloaded my free app, Real Talk Kim. On every social media platform, I am known as Real Talk Kim who is always telling you like it is. I do exactly what I would have wanted people to have done for me through my many seasons of rejection, denial, betrayal, and rebellion. I am reaching more beautiful people now than I could have ever dreamed because I began allowing those who could influence me to be honest with me. Now, it's up to you!

Loving you more than you know,
REAL TALK KIM

ACKNOWLEDGMENTS

There is no way I could have finished this book without so many amazing people in my life who have supported me through the toughest of times and the best of times—those people who inspire me and support me in each endeavor that I attempt. I am amazed at how the Holy Spirit gives me insight into new ideas for my ministry and then my tribe supports me until it's accomplished. This book could not be in existence today without those people whom I call family.

The two young men in my life who call me Mom will never know how much I love and appreciate their support. Morgan and Lyncoln, I am so very proud of the amazing, strong men you have become. I can't wait to see you as you walk in your purpose. Thank you for loving me as your mom even when I was unlovable.

Mom, we did it again. We were able to complete another book that has our hearts written on each page. You capture my heart as I deliver God's thoughts from online platforms to teaching and preaching sessions. You are my best friend, and I honor you for walking with me through my tough times as you were facing the loss of your love of fifty-two years, my dad. I honor Dr. Henry R. Jones, the man with a vision who had a heart for planting churches and loving God's people. I am pastoring the last church you two pastored before Dad passed to his forever home. He would be so proud of the woman I have become.

To Rob and Melissa, my brother and sister-in-love, I could not do life without you. You are critical in keeping me grounded and seeing the bigger picture as I, the visionary, explore new ministries and ventures. You allow me to be me as I cast vision that has not been explored in our realm and then support me as we make it work.

To our Real Talk Kim ministry team who orders my world—thank you for working day and night to see the reality of the vision come to pass. To our Limitless Church staff—thank you for blending ministries in so many areas and covering me as I carry the gospel to the nations weekly. To the Real Talk Kim Inner Circle—we have become a tight-knit family growing together and supporting each other in all areas of life.

To my Lord and Savior, Jesus Christ. Thank You so much for being my Lord and calling me to love Your people. Because You went to the cross for me and covered my sins, I realize the importance of being all that You have commissioned me to be.

ABOUT THE AUTHOR

Pastor Kimberly Jones, known as Real Talk Kim, travels the world fulfilling her passion and purpose of loving people back to life. She is a mother, pastor, entrepreneur, mentor, motivational speaker, entertainer, and bestselling author.

She is using her influence to mentor people all over the world through her mentorship program, RTK Inner Circle. Real Talk Kim is an advocate for GIVE Culture Foundation for Impact, a nonprofit organization that teaches mindfulness and generosity to the next generation of leaders.

Real Talk Kim has a successful weekly syndicated podcast and has appeared on *Preachers of Atlanta*, *The Dr. Oz Show*, *Chatter Talk Show*, BET, *Nightline*, and numerous podcasts, webinars, and radio programs.

Real Talk Kim is a true worshipper after God's own heart, a testament of God's redemption plan in action. She is the senior pastor at Limitless Church with campuses in Fayetteville and Atlanta, Georgia. She is the proud mother of two sons, Morgan and Lyncoln.